"Every writer in this anthol _____ _____ _____ a Soul Coach and each of these remarkab _____ ...en has an innate connection to the four elements through their work in this field. They truly make a difference in the world by dovetailing their understanding of the four elements and their practice as Soul Coaches into the immensely valuable information found in this anthology. May this book deepen your connection to the wonders of the natural world and to the truth of your soul."

—DENISE LINN, author of *Soul Coaching, 28 Days to Discover Your Authentic Self,* and Founder of Soul Coaching®
www.DeniseLinn.com

"As I read these stories, a calm entered my being and warmth rose in my heart. They helped me to feel a connection . . . connection to the authors of these stories, connection to the elements of Nature and most importantly, a connection back to the deepest part of my self. A beautiful book filled with ancient wisdom, whose time it is once again to share."

—MINNIE KANSMAN, Eco-Balance: Humanity in Harmony with Nature, Certified Feng Shui and Space Clearing Consultant and Teacher, and author of *Spirit Gardens: Rekindling our Nature Connection*
www.MinnieKansman.com

"Each chapter of *Soul Whispers II* leads us on our own journey of insight, healing and transformation. We are connected to a greater sense of being . . . delightfully, magically and joyfully. I came away feeling I had been blessed by wise women and gifted with Sacred Secrets."

—KIM PENTECOST, Sacred teacher, Intuitive and author/ coordinator for the anthology *The Wisdom We Have Gained*
www.WisdomGained.com and www.WisdomDance.com

SOUL WHISPERS II

Secret Alchemy of the Elements
in Soul Coaching

Soul Blessings,
Maura Clark

Edited by Sophia Fairchild

FOREWORD BY DENISE LINN
Author of *Soul Coaching,*
28 *Days to Discover Your Authentic Self*

SOUL WINGS® PRESS
Sydney, Australia
Laguna Beach, CA, USA

Library of Congress Cataloging-in-Publication Data
Soul Whispers II : secret alchemy of the elements in soul coaching / edited by Sophia Fairchild ; foreword by Denise Linn.
p. cm.
ISBN 9780984593002
1. Self-actualization (Psychology). 2. Self-actualization (Psychology) – Problems, exercises, etc. 3. Spiritual life – Anecdotes. 4. Spiritual life – Problems, exercises, etc. 5. Personal coaching. 6. Life skills. I. Soul whispers two : secret alchemy of the elements in soul coaching. II. Fairchild, Sophia. III. Linn, Denise. IV. Title.
BF637.P36   F35 2010   158.1 21—DC22   2010912072

Excerpts from *Soul Coaching Oracle Cards Guidebook* by Denise Linn, reprinted with permission from the author and Hay House, Inc. Carlsbad, CA. Copyright © 2005 by Denise Linn.

All names have been changed to protect client confidentiality, unless otherwise noted. The authors of this book do not dispense medical advice or prescribe the use of any technique as a form of treatment for physical or medical problems without the advice of a physician, either directly or indirectly. The intent of the editor and authors is only to offer information of a general nature to help you in your quest for emotional and spiritual well-being. In the event you use any of the information in this book for yourself, which is your personal right, the authors, editor and the publisher assume no responsibility for your actions.

The term Soul Coaching® is a Federally Registered Trademark and remains the property of Denise Linn Seminars, Inc. Wherever the term Soul Coaching® appears throughout this book the appropriate trademark symbol is implied.

Editorial Supervision by Sophia Fairchild
Book Design by Fiona Raven

First Printing January 2011
Printed in Canada

Published by Soul Wings® Press
Publishing for the Soul®
668 N Coast Hwy, Suite 234
Laguna Beach, CA 92651, USA
125 Oxford Street, Suite 125
Bondi Junction NSW 2022 Australia
www.SoulWingsPress.com

This book is dedicated
with love and gratitude to
Denise Linn
and to Soul Coaches
everywhere.

Contents

Foreword

The sound of the insistent early morning phone kept punctuating my dream. I wasn't ready to wake up. I knew that I was dreaming about something important but just when I thought that I was about to capture it, the phone would ring again. Reluctantly, I reached over and picked it up.

"I'm just calling to let you know that your grandmother has passed on," said the voice on the other end. The relative who called seemed to drone on, but I didn't really hear anything after the first sentence. I thanked the voice. Hung up. And then numbly stepped outside. Of course grandparents die. That's the nature of the cycle of life. But somehow I didn't expect this or plan on it. I thought my grandmother would be around forever.

I found myself climbing up to the top of a nearby hill. The sun wasn't up, but a storm was brewing in the wane light of east. The cold wind whipped my hair into my eyes. Images of my grandmother with her turkeys and the one feather she wore atop her head filled my heart as I watched jagged shards of lightening pummel the earth. My heart was heavy with grief.

My grandmother was Cherokee as was my grandfather, who had already died. Their world was alive with Spirit. Spirit was everywhere. It was in the wild colors of the sunset. It was in the scent of newly sown hay and in the warmth of winter sun filtering through a window on a frosty morning. They understood that a living spirit flowed through all things. They had an innate understanding of the natural forces that shaped their world.

I watched the approach of the storm. One drop. Then another. The sharp, bracing rain pounded my body, but I didn't move. Then, just a quickly as it arrived, the storm passed and sunlight flooded the land. The grass looked greener than I remembered and the air smelled fresher. There wasn't the ubiquitous rainbow that always seems to accompany the passing of someone dear, but there was something even more precious in the wake of the storm. There was a feeling of renewal.

The power of the wind, the water from the pelting rain, the warmth of the fire of the sun and the green bounty of the earth that was so vibrant after the storm — all of these things renewed and replenished my soul. I felt cleansed by the elements and I was at peace with my grandmother's death. In a mystical kind of way, the storm and the elements of nature activated an inner knowing of the truth that my grandmother was not dead, but had only passed to what my family called "the happy hunting grounds."

Throughout history, the elements – air, water, fire and earth – have been associated with healing, natural balance and wholeness. Ancient and native people knew that within each element were patterns of energy that permeated the universe. They used this understanding to develop cosmological models to create a sense of harmony in their lives. From Native Americans to ancient Greeks, Egyptians, Mayans, Aztecs, Persians, Celts, and Hindus, the mysterious panorama of nature has been divided into separate parts that are designated by the four elements. Egyptian sages fervently believed that reflecting upon the four elements provided a profound understanding of life. In the mystery schools of Mesopotamia, initiates underwent rigorous rites of Air, Water, Fire, and Earth to test particular aspects of their natures. Hippocrates, honored as the father of medicine, declared that a patient's health depended upon a balance of the four elements.

My grandparents died before I designed the Soul Coaching® 28-Day Program; however I felt their spirit flow through me as I created it. I knew that the same elemental forces that helped harmonize the lives of my ancestors (and so many native and ancient people) could, in an almost mystical way, bring life into harmony for others. Hence, the four element aspect of Soul Coaching® was born.

Each of the four weeks of the Soul Coaching® 28-Day Program is assigned an element, and during that week the element is a backdrop for the exercises done during the week. For example, the second week is focused on emotional healing and the element is water (which traditionally has been associated with our emotional state). During the week, as you are examining your emotions, you also pay particular attention to the water that you drink, the water with which you cleanse yourself, and the water in the natural world – the rain, streams and oceans. In an alchemical way, the elements profoundly deepen the exercises in this program.

Every writer in this anthology has trained with me to become a Soul Coach and each of these remarkable women has an innate connection to the four elements through their work in this field. In this anthology, they have dovetailed their understanding of the elements and their practice as Soul Coaches into immensely valuable information that you can use in your life. The Creator always sends me the best people and I have been blessed to have these women in my life. They are truly making a difference in the world. My additional kudos to their splendid editor, Sophia Fairchild. Through her gentle nudging and kindness, honed with the clarity of her editing skills, each of these stories has been polished and blessed. Enjoy!

May the power of the Air, Water, Fire and Earth bring blessings into your life and may this book deepen your connection to the wonders of the natural world and to the truth of your soul.

DENISE LINN
Founder of Soul Coaching®

Introduction

That which is below is like that which is above,
that which is above is like that which is below,
to perform the miracles of the one thing.

These words are said to have been inscribed on the Emerald Tablet, known as *The Secret of Secrets*, attributed to the Egyptian Hermes Trismegistus and recorded for posterity in a letter from Socrates to Alexander the Great.

In the notion "as above, so below," *above* represents the universe and *below* represents oneself. Like the yin-yang symbol, each lies within the other. Thus by understanding one we may begin to understand the other, and thereby gain an understanding of the whole. Indigenous wisdom expresses this best as "everything is interconnected."

The Emerald Tablet text became an important reference point for alchemists from medieval and renaissance times through to Carl G. Jung in the past century, since it was believed to contain the secrets of enlightenment.

At its heart, alchemy is the process of transforming our mundane human consciousness (lead) into spiritual consciousness (gold). The result of this transformational process is the discovery of the mythical 'Philosopher's Stone' (enlightenment).

The mythological definition of an alchemist is someone who takes something lacking in apparent value and turns it into something of great worth. In the traditional allegory, the alchemist takes lead and, working with various elements, turns it into gold.

We could go further and view this symbolic substance, lead, as something which is not particularly life-enhancing, something which is weighing us down. This could be seen as anything which stifles our life force or holds us back from fulfilling our highest potential.

Instead of ignoring, avoiding or discarding this material, the alchemist uses this leaden substance as the raw material from which to create a magical transformation. After all, without raw material the alchemist would have nothing with which to work.

By using the analogy of alchemy in our own lives, we can take our perceived problems (the lead) and view them as opportunities for growth (raw material) thus transforming them into inspired breakthroughs in our personal awareness and new life force. This leads us on to living a fulfilled life at our highest potential (the gold).

Like alchemy, Soul Coaching® is a self-initiated process of transformation through the four elements. These four elements, Air, Water, Fire and Earth, have, since ancient times, been connected with balance, harmony and healing. They provide us with a time-honored pathway to follow, a journey which opens and expands our awareness, offering a sense of sacredness to our everyday lives.

This collection of writing by experienced Soul Coaches gathered from all over the world invites you to listen to the whispers of the four elements as they speak to your soul, guiding you towards your true life direction, allowing you to create a life of deep meaning and joy.

Soul Coaching® takes you on a journey through the four elements directly to your spiritual source, at the same time providing a comprehensive system for deciphering their whispered messages. With each element you explore, something new is activated within you.

As Denise Linn explains, Soul Coaching® is a remarkable program designed for anyone seeking phenomenal spiritual cleansing, renewal and transformation. Its aim is to align one's inner spiritual life with their outer life. It helps to clear away mental, emotional and physical clutter, so your client can hear the secret messages from his or her soul. It also allows your client to discover their true purpose, so they can design a life that supports that purpose.

· Soul Coaching® goes beyond the boundaries of ordinary life coaching which focuses on the attainment of goals. It is also not a type of emotional therapy. Soul Coaching® is a guided inward journey to touch the sacred space within.

Every Soul Coach knows that their clients are naturally intuitive and resourceful, and understands that each client already has all the answers he or she needs. It is job of the Soul Coach to create a safe, nurturing space for their clients to discover their own knowledge, while they listen with their heart as well as their ears.

Soul Coaches work in several ways. They may take their clients on inner meditative journeys called Soul Journeys to receive profound answers to heartfelt questions. They can also gently guide their clients through a 28 day program that is a deep inner and outer clutter clearing of the mental, emotional, physical and spiritual aspects of Self, a journey represented by the Medicine Wheel and the ancient elements of Air, Water, Fire and Earth. This 28 day program may also be followed by quiet time spent alone on a personal Quest.

Some of the reported side effects of this alchemical journey are mental clarity, renewed passion and creativity, the release of outworn beliefs, increased intuition, the healing of emotional wounds, enhanced self-image, healed relationships, a sense of compassion and community, and an awareness of the light at the core of the soul.

Each Soul Coach represented in *Soul Whispers II* brings a unique approach to their Soul Coaching® practice, based on years of knowledge and skill in many different professional fields.

The variety of distinctive voices, the depth of expertise, the wealth of practical exercises and personal sacred ceremony shared here is truly remarkable! May you be inspired to listen for the whispered wisdom of the elements as you read these stories.

By journeying through the pages of this book, you are invited to become an initiate into the secret alchemical process of the elements, to deepen your authentic connection with the true path of your soul.

May your journey be blessed!

SOPHIA FAIRCHILD
Sydney, Australia

In powerful and often mysterious ways, the effects of this program will manifest in your life for years to come.

—DENISE LINN

HELEN MUMFORD SOLE
New York, USA

HELEN MUMFORD SOLE spent over 20 years in business, holding senior positions in large companies including Senior Vice President of Gartner and CEO of LexisNexis UK. She also created several successful startups.

For most of this time, Helen was searching for ways to get more in touch with her inner voice. She discovered techniques to liberate her talents and those of her colleagues, and coaching her team became one of the most enjoyable aspects of her job.

One day, Helen realized that the dream she was living was not her own, signalling a major life change.

These days Helen is a coach and energy therapist practicing in Old Greenwich, Connecticut and Manhattan, New York. She is also a happiness coach, teaching classes and speaking regularly on the subject. Her clients are often executives who feel that something is missing, are wondering what to do next, or looking for ways to become more inspired and achieve their potential in their current roles. She also practices Reiki and other energy and crystal therapies.

Helen lives in Manhattan with her husband and a variable number of their many children. Helen is passionate about global charity Merlin (Medical Emergency Relief International) who provide desperately needed healthcare in some of the most difficult places in the world. She is honoured to sit on their Board.

Helen holds a Bachelor's and Master's degree from Oxford University, is a certified Soul Coach, Reiki Master/Teacher, and crystal therapist.

Contact her at www.LoveandGratitude.com

Elementary, My Dear Watson:
Bringing the Four Elements of Your Life Into Harmony

HELEN MUMFORD SOLE

It was only when I had journeyed through each of the four elements in turn that I understood and felt what real connection and balance can be.

I now realize that Ancient Wisdom completely passed me by for the first 35 years of my life. Even had I known about the four element theory that is so well documented by Buddhist and Hindu philosophers and historians, it would not have made any difference because I'd have been 100% confident that, while they might apply to everyone else, they certainly didn't apply to me.

The rules I lived under instead would be better characterized as:

- *Faster is always better than slower*
- *Why wait until tomorrow when there's today?*
- *Impatience is a virtue*
- *Why take the scenic route when there's a shortcut?*
- *Instant gratification almost always beats delayed gratification*

I might add that I also believed in thinner, richer, louder, bigger, better, faster, and more, more, more.

I was the sort of person who would start a book and then read the end because I wanted to find out what happened without having to plough through the middle. I would start weight loss diets but only do the really extreme bits at the beginning where you shed the pounds very quickly. What I did, I did excellently, but I was always in a hurry and always on a mission. And I never understood or bought into the Aesop's Fable about the tortoise and the hare.

As a consequence of these beliefs and this impatience, I was driven, focused, great fun, and very successful. I got married in my mid-twenties to a good and handsome man who loved me, and I loved him. We had two wonderful children, and we lived in a fabulous house with our black Labrador in the Home Counties in England.

My career was always in excellent shape. Among other things, I held very senior positions in global companies, as well as doing startups and raising venture capital.

My life was rich and varied, and I traveled the world meeting interesting and influential people. In short, my rules were working pretty well, and I was living the dream. If I'd known about Ancient Wisdom and the four elements, I'd have said I didn't need them, because everything was going swimmingly and nothing needed to change.

Unfortunately, after a while, it turned out that the dream I was living was not my own. Something was missing. The only rhythm in my life was of acceleration. I was hurtling along at breakneck speed. Work took up too much time, and when I wasn't working I was with my two young children or sleeping. I'd lost any kind of connection with the natural ebb and flow of the world, the universe, my family, and my body. Looking back I was deeply unhappy and getting increasingly out of balance and out of touch.

While everything on the surface was apparently wonderful, deep down I was floundering. I'd lost touch with my inner voice, and I could no longer hear my soul and the truth that it was whispering.

If only I'd understood the Ancient Wisdom of the four elements, I'd have realized that my life was way out of balance and that I needed to bring the mental (Air), emotional (Water), spiritual (Fire), and physical (Earth) aspects of my life back into harmony and peaceful equilibrium.

If I had known then what I know now, I could have put myself through the Soul Coaching program. By following the program diligently, I would have brought the four aspects of my nature into focus and could have made some serious and life-changing discoveries. Maybe I could have achieved in 28 days what it eventually took me more than 10 turbulent years to accomplish!

There's no escaping the truth of Ancient Wisdom. Happiness lies in the fulfillment that comes from achieving balance among your mental, spiritual, emotional, and physical planes. Thinking it doesn't apply to you is no defense. Believing you can somehow buck the system and just major in one of the four elements isn't going to do it in the long term – believe me, I tried this for years. Choosing to quiet the little voice inside your head that's telling you something's not right is not a long-term strategy. Ancient Wisdom means it applies to you too, and if you don't hear the whispers, you're going to hear the screams.

And so began my long and incredibly rewarding tour of the four elements.

The first of the four elements to surround me and demand my attention was Air. Air remains my favorite element to this day and represents mental clarity. When I feel overwhelmed by everything that I have to think about and do, I return to Air. When I'm being indecisive and unclear in my thoughts and direction I look to Air. When I focus on the Air element and physically declutter my world, I find that the cobwebs and shadows in my mind miraculously spring loose, and I emerge feeling mentally fresh and clear and ready for anything.

Back in the late '90s, I was a long way from mental clarity. My mind was overly full with the day-to-day activities of the company I had helped to found and been instrumental in growing. Looking back, that small four-year-old company of about 30 people had taken over my life and hijacked my happiness. I didn't particularly enjoy the business or the culture, but I'd invested a considerable amount of money in the startup and, as chief operating officer, I was responsible for its growth and success. I felt shackled to the company and my identity had become intertwined with that of the organization.

After a few more years, we had groomed the company for sale. We found several potential buyers and after the most intense period of work imaginable, we finally completed the sale.

Looking back, I can now see that with the sale of the company, a huge mental and physical decluttering took place. As the company moved its offices to those of the new owner, we helped the removal people pack up our files and records. Anything that wasn't important was jettisoned. Much of the paper and other records that we'd carefully accumulated over all that time got piled into recycling bags. It felt as though the history of the company had been reduced to a set of packing boxes and a collection of laptops.

The reality was that the value of the company we had sold was not in the stuff (the e-mails, reports, accounts and contracts) but was actually in the quality and expertise of the staff and the personal relationships we had with our customers.

It was a metaphor for life, really. I made a lot of money from the sale of that company, but the real value of that time for me is not the money but the expertise and experience I gained while I was there, as well as some strong relationships that were forged through both the good and the bad times.

This decluttering had the effect of lifting the fog from my brain. I felt I could function again. Although I still worked and held a senior position in the company that had acquired us, I began to look beyond the four walls of the office. I wasn't tired all the time, and my powers of concentration for matters outside of work increased dramatically. I began to read books again and enjoy my family and friends. I took up horseback riding and weekly French lessons, and I began the slow process of unwinding from the intensity of the old environment.

The decluttering of the office started the process, and as the old building was closed and the company took on the name of the new owners, the process became complete. Air had blown through my business life and cleared my head. Mental clarity was once more my own, and the business of living became richer and more enjoyable.

While this felt like the end of something, it was, of course, only the beginning. Whereas the old me would have thought I could just "do" the Air element bit and not bother with Water, Fire, or Earth, obviously Ancient Wisdom knows better, and so with this new mental clarity came the glimmer of another perspective. I began to get in touch with an inner voice and hear the gentle, though still faraway, whispers of my soul. I became aware of a curiosity bubbling up in my head and body insisting that I explore the spiritual side of my nature, which had been overlooked for most of my life.

This was the call of Fire, the element that clears the shadows and links us with our spiritual selves.

It always surprises me that Fire is the element of spirituality. Fire conjures up images of something hot, violent, and explosive. My experience with Fire has been anything but that. It has been the calmest and most peaceful of my journeys, and that serenity continues to this day.

It all started with weekly Reiki sessions. Reiki is a Japanese energy therapy that balances the chakras and produces a sense of deep relaxation, which in turn promotes healing. My Reiki sessions moved my soul, re-energized my body, and left me feeling light and buoyant. Even my family noticed the difference and said I was a nicer person after every treatment! The lightness I felt, and the fact that the rest of my family were also benefiting, encouraged me to attend regularly. After a few months, I knew that I wanted to be able to give Reiki as well as receive it, so I signed up for a class.

Pretty soon I was being trained myself, and about five energy-filled years later I became a Master/Teacher in Usui Reiki. My thirst for spirituality remained strong, and I qualified to the same Master/Teacher level in Karuna and Komyo Reiki and then became an Advanced Integrated Energy Therapist. Meanwhile I was reading extensively on all aspects of spirituality, spent a weekend with a Buddhist monk, and weeks with energy workers in Sedona. I became trained in Transcendental Meditation, qualified as a crystal healer and a past-life regression therapist, and of course received my certification as a Soul Coach.

So Fire was and continues to be a peaceful journey for me, with lots of sparks of interest and learning, but no unpleasant flames or eruptions!

I think the Ancient Wisdom knew what it was doing by warming me with the Fire element before showering me with Water! Water is the element of the emotional self. It connects and bathes you in the glow of your true emotions and brings forth emotional balance. My experience with Water is truly the most tur-bulent and hard-won transition of my life so far.

Following two years of Air and a couple more years of Fire, my soul was again whispering. This time I could hear it loudly and clearly. It was an insistent voice and it said that I wasn't happy, that my time with my first husband was nearly over. We'd been together for 13 years, and built a good life with our two children. Our marriage had generally been happy and fulfilling and we'd been close friends and partners in the journey of life. The fact is that the new me, enlightened by my experiences, had fallen in love with someone else, a fact that was as shocking to me as it was to my husband.

For almost a year we attempted to stay together. I gave up my career com-pletely to spend time in the home with my husband and children. I did weekly psychotherapy sessions and worked hard to understand myself, my relationships with my birth family, and my marriage. I wanted to discover a way to put the genie back in the bottle and repair and rebuild my marriage, but it wasn't to be. My desire to leave couldn't be contained, and amid much sorrow and tears my husband and I called it a day. We tried to make sure the process of separation and divorce was as gentle as possible for the children, and while we had our moments, I'm proud that we worked everything out ourselves and resolved all our issues without recourse to lawyers and acrimony in the divorce courts.

It was an October day in 2003 when I finally left the marital home. It was a sad day for us all, and I remember lying in bed that night, and for many nights afterwards, missing my husband like mad. How can it be, I thought, that I can be so pleased to be with someone, and so distraught not to be with someone else?

My decision was a good one though. I married my second husband in 2004, and our baby daughter was born later that year. My first husband also happily remarried, and his new son was born two months after our daughter.

I emerged in 2005 from a traumatic couple of years and felt emotionally drained by the turbulence and pain of ending my first marriage, and at the same time soothed and calmed by the certainty with which I had entered my second marriage. With Air, Fire, and Water now more balanced and connected than ever before, it was inevitable that, unbeknownst to me, the Earth element was now beckoning urgently.

Earth is devoted to the strengthening and protection of your physical self, and given the traumas of the preceding years, it was time for me to address myself physically.

It's not surprising that many people become seriously ill within three years of going through a divorce. Having been divorced, started a new job, moved house, remarried, had a miscarriage, and given birth to a healthy baby, you can imagine that I was not in the best physical condition.

I'd rather taken my health for granted during my first 35 years, but following my initial encounter with Air back in the late '90s and the mental clarity that had followed, I'd given up both drinking alcohol and smoking tobacco thank goodness. During my Fire moments of spiritual connection I'd taken up Ashtanga yoga and loved it, but one of the consequences of my marital problems was that I'd stopped doing yoga and started drinking wine again. I'd found it difficult to sleep during that year and often survived on just four hours each night. Eventually, I'd gone back to work so that I could provide for myself and the children, and was the CEO of a large company. It was a demanding job and engaged a great deal of my attention, deflecting me from any possibility of exercise or healthy diet.

My pregnancies were the best thing that could have happened for my health. As always I took them very seriously, giving up alcohol and eating super-healthily. Slowly, I regained my ability to sleep at night and life calmed down a little. After my baby was born, I needed to lose some weight and regain muscle tone and hired a personal trainer with whom I did cardiovascular work and weights. This helped enormously and got me into better physical shape but still left me yearning for something else. I felt better, but there was still something missing.

It was after we moved to the U.S. that I found what I was searching for. By this time, I had a thriving coaching and energy practice and was fortunate to meet a lady who had survived several life-threatening cancers. As part of her journey she was learning about food and nutrition and introduced me to macrobiotics. The principle of eating balanced food that is fresh and as close to living as possible, that's in season and avoids animal products, held great appeal. I employed a wonderful coach to teach me the principles and practices of this style of eating and with the help and support of my husband and two teenage children, set about preparing food in that way.

We all immediately felt better than we had for years. We found it easier to get up in the morning and had more than enough energy to last us through our busy days. A list of minor ailments slowly dissolved during the course of the following 12 months. My interest in all nutritional matters increased and, as well as receiving coaching and attending conferences and training courses on macrobiotics, we also became completely vegan. This marked another step change in our health. I lost weight and began to glow with health and vitality. The Earth element had done its work and I felt physically awake and well.

> ### Fulfillment
>
> *AFFIRMATION: Joy abounds in all areas of my life.*
>
> *Deep satisfaction and emotional contentment will be unfolding in your life! Soon you will be reaping inner and outer riches and opportunities! Honor your success, and enjoy the fruits of your labor.*

Most importantly, I now felt closely in touch with the physical, mental, emotional, and spiritual aspects of my nature, all at the same time. I was conscious of having mental clarity, of feeling emotionally very balanced with no disturbances to my peace and calm. I knew that my spiritual practices were more focused and that the energy work I did with my clients was even stronger and more effective.

It was only when I had journeyed through each of the four elements in turn that I understood and felt what real connection and balance can be. It is only when we have addressed our mental, emotional, spiritual, and physical selves that we are liberated and can be our best.

Which brings us to today. Of course, I'm still very much a work in progress. Every day I reflect on some aspect of the four elements and look consciously for opportunities to connect with them.

Right now, I'm sitting here at my desk looking out at the ocean, which is about twenty yards away. The presence of water in my life is a continual reminder of the importance of my emotional self. I watch the tides ebb and flow and remember that the steady rhythm of life is the only constant.

We spend every winter weekend up in the mountains in Vermont. Skiing called me late in life. I'd never even put a pair of skis on my feet until I was 43. I think I understand why I love the mountains so much. Air is my favorite element, and I never feel closer and more in touch with Air than when I'm in the mountains. I breathe deeply and know that life is good. It's so pure, so crisp, so clarifying. It clears my head of everything and puts me back in touch with my essence. It's like a weekly mental decluttering and leaves me feeling revived and refreshed.

My spirituality continues to grow. The treatment room where I work with my clients has one wall made up almost entirely of glass and looks south over Long Island Sound. We are blessed with a clear climate here, and most days the room is filled with sunshine and warmth. I do my formal spiritual practice in this room whether it's with my clients or alone. As I see the sun glinting off the water and feel the rays on my skin, I feel connected to the Fire element. I get closer and closer to my spiritual essence and feel empowered to take my clients with me. My daily practice is spiritually based, and I incorporate meditation, gratitude journaling, and spending time in nature into my schedule every day. As the product of a religious background, I love my return to spirituality. The softness and inner peace and calm that permeate my life as a consequence enhance my ability to love and be loved.

Most days, I shop for fresh produce so I can connect myself and my family with the Earth. The old me disliked cooking intensely. Nowadays, I spend about two hours a day buying and preparing food for my family. And I love it. I am better nourished than ever, and feel the rhythm of the seasons through the ripeness of the grains, legumes and vegetables that I lovingly select and prepare.

On the surface, my life really isn't so different from how it was before. I'm still busy, and still a little impatient. My husband loves me, and I love him. My children are teenagers and beginning to leave home. My youngest is old enough to have started kindergarten. Although I'm calmer and more peaceful, I'm still driven and focused . . . and life is great fun.

I can see the impact of the Ancient Wisdom of the four elements everywhere I look, yet our lives are thoroughly modern and mainstream. I'm just happier, balanced, more connected and grounded . . . and I can hear the whispers.

Whether you do it in 28 days as part of a soul coaching program or whether you do it over 10 years or more as I did, I recommend that you get to know Air, Water, Fire, and Earth and make them your friends. Whatever you're looking for, they will help you to find it. Whatever your soul is whispering to you, they will help you to hear it.

How to Listen to your Soul

Your soul is in constant communication with you. There are many words to describe that little voice inside us and depending on the message, we call it our *conscience, intuition, inspiration, instinct, sixth sense* and so on.

As you get more and more out of balance, your ability to hear your soul is reduced. As you race off down the path to disequilibrium, even if you can still hear this voice, your willingness to listen to it declines significantly. Just when you need it the most, you are cut off from the inner wisdom of your soul.

But your soul continues to speak, and from time to time you hear the faint whisper of something inside of yourself. You feel the vague discomfort of knowing that something isn't quite right. The longer you ignore these feelings and the longer you put off their resolution, the bigger the resulting crisis can be. Your soul never stops communicating with you and if you don't listen to the whispers, then you're going to hear the screams.

The first step therefore is to start listening to your soul. Getting in touch with your soul is simply a matter of habit. It's not difficult; it's just something that needs a little time and awareness. Eventually it becomes routine.

Step 1 – How to Listen to your Soul

- Find a quiet time; sit down and do nothing except let your thoughts ramble.

- Be aware of what you're thinking without judging, critiquing or criticizing your thoughts in any way.

- Make a note of any recurring themes.

- Ideally do this daily, but weekly or monthly are also good places to start.

- Every time you have any experience of that little voice inside you, embrace it before you dismiss it. Write it down.

- If ever you encounter the discomfort of knowing that something isn't quite right, acknowledge it before you discard it, and notice if it keeps coming back to you. If you can, capture this knowledge in a note book.

I find that meditating helps me to get in touch with my inner self. When I meditate I'm much more able to hear my inner voice in my everyday life, so I strongly recommend a regular meditation practice.

Step 2 – Deciding which Messages need Action

Sorting out the underlying issues from everyday stresses, strains and the discomforts of life is not always easy. The fact that you've had a bad day at the office doesn't necessarily mean it's time to change your career. You shouldn't put your house up for sale just because you're having a little difficulty with a neighbor. So how can you determine which are the whispers of our souls, and which are simply the terrier-like thoughts of your mind playing with the events of the day?

This is where it's very useful to become familiar with any process involving the Four Element theory of Ancient Wisdom. If you understand which part of your life your soul is whispering about, instead of trying to tackle a specific issue, you can address an entire area. This is a more gentle approach and delivers much more rounded, holistic and complete results. It also means that you don't mix up your soul whispers with the random thoughts of your mind.

- When you examine your list of possible soul whispers, look for any recurring themes or trends.

- When you have identified the themes or trends, decide which areas of your life they relate to. It doesn't matter if you're not sure, just do your best.

- Classify each into one or more of the following categories:

Anything related to your body or physical self	Earth
To do with your emotions and how you feel about something or someone (including yourself)	Water
Concerning mental uncertainty or fogginess	Air
Relating to your spiritual nature	Fire

Step 3 – Taking Action

Based on the results of Step 2, decide which of the four elements to start working with. If you're not sure, just go for whichever one feels right for you. If you still can't decide, start with Air. I find the accomplishment of Air's mental clarity gives me the release and energy to do anything!

You can start at any time. Your soul is whispering to you now . . .

ULRIKE BEHRE-BRANDES

Gelsenkirchen, Germany

Ulrike Behre-Brandes lives a busy family life in Gelsenkirchen, Germany. Meeting Denise Linn and attending her seminars since 1993 has been a turning point in her life. In August 2003 Ulrike Behre-Brandes was personally certified in Soul Coaching® by Denise Linn.

As a Certified Soul Coach® her goal is to inspire people to find their own inspiration, their own expression and to find a place of creativity within themselves. She holds a safe space for her clients, to make it easier for them to connect with who they really are. This is what makes her heart sing! She is an expert in supporting women during their menopause passage. Ulrike loves to assist people integrating the Soul Coaching® tools into their daily routine, so they can live their ordinary life with extraordinary possibilities.

Her background includes energy work with Sion R. Windelov, movement work with Gabrielle Roth (5 Rhythms), training in meditation with Petra Schneider and traveling worldwide studying people and cultures.

Ulrike runs seminars, workshops and holds lectures on a variety of topics. She is also involved with primary education. Ulrike Behre-Brandes is co-author of *Soul Whispers: Collective Wisdom from Soul Coaches around the World,* Soul Wings® Press 2009. Contact Ulrike at bebra50@hotmail.com

For further information visit: www.SoulCoaching-BehreBrandes.de

Live Your Ordinary Life
with Extraordinary Possibilities

ULRIKE BEHRE-BRANDES

The whole universe is abundance. It is everywhere; it is unlimited.

The world is changing very fast and for many people this can be a time of great uncertainty. Since the global financial crisis (starting in 2008) most of us have begun to realize that the old ways are not sustainable any more. We cannot go on with the old *more-more-me-me-want-want-need-need* sort of philosophy. It needs to be changed. Many people are looking for a way to achieve more harmony within themselves and with the world. They are searching for a depth of who they are.

On the other hand, there are people who get more and more involved in the fear and the drama in the world. It is our choice, which way we want to go. From one perspective it can look scarier, more painful and more dramatic. But from another perspective there is more hope, more support and there are more possibilities. If we focus on the creation of choice then we will be more open-minded to new ideas of sustainability, new ideas of working together and the idea of remembering who we really are.

"How can I do this? How can I make it a daily practice in my life? Where do I start?" I have been asked these questions hundreds of times. My answer is always the same. Join me for a 28-day Soul Coaching program. The different weekly exercises and meditations will take you on a journey of transformation. During this journey you are getting rid of old past dramas and you will clear old blockages. So by taking this next step, it will be a more intuitive, empowered, action-orientated movement into your future.

From my own experience, the 28-day Soul Coaching program is a very intensive and most effective group program. It consists of six evening classes (2 hour sessions) with a follow-up group evaluation session one month after completion. The specific energy of a group supports this program of mental, emotional, spiritual and physical cleansing in a very special way. I think the group members always meet for a special reason and not by chance. To make it practical, to make it real in their lives, the participants support each other when doing the daily self- examination tasks. So it is easier for them to integrate these tasks into their lives. To make it even more practical, these tasks are divided into three levels, depending on the time you have available. No matter how busy you are or how hectic your life is, you can complete the program.

I am sure that Soul Coaching groups show us a new way of working together. It is this synergistic energy of a group of people working together that shows us we are not separated from each other. It is that feeling of supporting each other which encourages a sense of community and cooperation which is electrifying. Maybe this is one of the new possibilities for our future life: to become a greater community that supports each other by working together, a combined energy that helps to intensify the results. And this is not just an intellectual philosophy. It is about making it practical for your everyday life.

The most wonderful thing about Soul Coaching is that this journey will provide you with the context and conditions you need to make positive changes in your life and in your personal development. But what happens if you are scared of change? The good news is: it doesn't matter whether you like change or not, whether you embrace it or run in the opposite direction. Not only will changes be taking place, they will be taking place all the time, with or without your full participation. Your choice is to take steps forward towards change, or to wait and see what surprises the universe has for you while you are clinging to what you thought was safety. So why don't you choose to create the most empowered and graceful path forward in alignment with your soul's yearnings?

This is what more and more people are opening up to, people from different backgrounds with all different kinds of learning attitudes. A Certified Soul Coach can help you make a fresh start, to remember who you really are. He or she will hold a safe space and will be present with each person. A coach won't try to change you from your philosophy but will find the best way for the Soul Coaching program to work for you; how he or she can assist to clear blockages or past dramas. This allows participants to move into the next step in a more intuitive and empowered way.

I can say from experience that doing the Soul Coaching program so many times over recent years that it has become a way of life for me. Once you have embarked on this journey of choosing authenticity, it will never end. That does not mean you don't have any challenges to face, but your reaction will be different. Putting your deepest self in the center of your existence will influence your environment, touch the people around you and most of all, affect your perception of yourself. Once you move forward, there is no turning back.

Old limitations, negative patterns and barriers will probably turn up several times again before they begin to drop away. When this happens our first reaction is judgment or resistance, because judgment is just a form of resistance. *Oh, no! Not this again! I have been through this so many times! I don't want this anymore!* But if you judge something you cannot get rid of it! If you think it will never come back again then you are not really free of it. All of the great teachers have taught the same thing. Whether you take the perspective of Christ, that of unconditional love or that of the Buddha, of non-attachment and compassion, or of the philosopher Lao Tse where everything is what it is; all the perspectives are of the same quality.

I invite you to try this mini Soul Journey with me if you want to let go of an old pattern that keeps occurring in your life. You may use it for any pattern you wish.

No matter what is occurring in your life right now, put yourself in a very still and quiet place. This can be a juicy green, sunny meadow, bathed in sunlight, or a warm sandy beach. Choose whichever feels good for you. Take a few deep breaths and relax. Bring your awareness into the present place and time. Know that all is well. All is well. Relax and let go. There is a place beneath the surface that is still and serene; a place that knows all is well. Sink into that place. Breathe and relax.

Think of a pattern in your life, something that keeps occurring. Be aware of it! Feel it! Take a few deep breaths now. Can you let it go now? Is it time for it to be over? You are free if you choose it now! This old pattern! Let it come to you like a bird on your hand. What does the bird look like? Take your time to look at it. Love it as it is. Allow it to be free now! Set it free now, so it can fly like a Phoenix into the sun. Allow it to fly like a Phoenix into the sun! Breathe. Breathe in and breathe out. All is well.

All is energy. You cannot destroy it, but you can allow it to change. Allow it to change. If you allow it to happen then it can happen! Love and embrace all things as they are and trust. Trust that this old pattern turns into a blessing with grace! All is well now. Take a deep breath. In this moment, choose unconditional love for yourself if that pattern ever returns again. Trust that all is well now; all is going to work out fine!

Take a few deep breaths. Good! Count to ten and slowly and gently open your eyes. Stretching now . . . Give yourself a big hug. You deserve it!

Abundance issues are another area where a shift in perspective can help to reveal that abundance is already everywhere. Abundance is about consciousness, the consciousness of who you are.

Have you ever looked into a baby's eyes? It is as if you look into the universe. You can see the universe in them. That's where we come from! That's what we all are part of! But many people still feel the energy of fear or lack in regards to wealth and health and happiness. On a deep level that means *I am not good enough to be loved, to be accepted, honored, cared for, wealthy*, etc. This comes from the mind; its origin is mental. The mind is always searching for the next thing. From the mind's point of view there is never enough. No matter how much you have, it still wants more. Try not to go shopping for two weeks . . . for many of us this is a drama.

Abundance is not about money; this is only a small part of it. Abundance is about life. So if you want to live in abundance consciousness, forget about money and open yourself to a bigger picture.

There is an abundance of air around you; there is an abundance of light, of dark, of trees, of animals, of leaves, of cars, of cities, of stones, of streets, of stars, of clouds, of cells in your body etc. From this point of view, can you tell me where there is no abundance? The whole universe is abundance. It is everywhere; it is unlimited.

The best way to integrate something is to acknowledge it and be grateful for it. So go around and observe the abundance all around you! *Oh, there is an abundance of stones, of flowers, of water in the garden. Thank you for this abundance!* Every time you notice it, you acknowledge it. Every time you acknowledge it, it becomes real for you, you feel it and then you are grateful for it. So this consciousness of abundance integrates into your consciousness. Use your imagination for a moment. For one week, simply go around and notice and acknowledge abundance and be grateful for this. How would you feel after this week? You would be living in it!

The universal law is: what you hold in your consciousness is what you attract. So you can attract an abundance of opportunities, an abundance of creativity, of friends, of health and maybe an abundance of money. But don't focus too much on the money. If you associate abundance with just money, it soon gets sticky because there are so many mental associations with money. Once you are holding this consciousness of abundance, you will feel it and you will live in it. Once it is integrated into your being, you can apply it in many situations of your life. All it takes is a little practice. How would your life be then? You would be more open to opportunities, creativity and there would be more peace in your mind.

Another aspect of abundance relates to supply. In the beginning, all the material things in this world came from the earth and the energy of the sun. Earth and sun give us the raw materials for everything. What do they charge us? This enormous supply is free of charge! So if you really think about it, there is so much abundance in every moment. Take your consciousness to the source and feel and open yourself up to the abundance already given to you. Be grateful for this! If you open to that, how can you feel that there is not enough for you? How can you feel a lack or the tightness of holding on? Practice holding an abundance consciousness for 15 minutes a day. From personal experience I can say, you will be living in much greater peace, inspiration will flow in more easily and you will find yourself living in abundance. All you have to do is practice it; be in the energy of it; be in the feeling of it. Make it practical, as a real possibility for your life, and enjoy it!

Remember that there is the word 'dance' in abundance. So feel free to create a dance while you are singing: "Come on money, hang out with me. I love you!" But don't take it too seriously or get too attached to it. There is no guarantee that this will cure your bank account, but feeling a lot of stress about it doesn't cure it either. Somebody once said: "Worrying is praying for what you don't want."

If you practice an abundance consciousness then you change your inner knowledge and attitude about it. When you are holding on to it consciously, the universe will begin to support this, but you have to hold it and feel it first. It has to be real! At the end of this chapter there is a simple exercise that I have found very effective for practicing abundance consciousness.

Sometimes it happens that you may need more help when dealing with the particular abundance issue you have. In this case I suggest you contact a Soul Coach for the support you need, especially if your issue relates to a past life experience. By exploring your past lives you may discover why you seem to sabotage yourself when it comes to success and abundance. A Soul Coach can create a perfect Soul Journey for you to visit your past lives with a purpose in mind. When you are doing the Soul Coaching program by yourself, I suggest listening to the wonderful short Soul Journeys Denise Linn has created on Hay House Radio. Just look into the show archives to find the right ones concerning abundance. Everyone holds an individual perception. So feel free to do what resonates with your soul.

As we can read in numerous recent articles, there will be an acceleration of energy in the future, which has already begun. In many ways the years to come will be important for us as individuals and as a collective. Denise Linn tells in her *January Newsletter* 2010: "We are co-creating our reality. Our thoughts will become our new reality with increasing speed." Everything that you desire strongly will manifest in your life, because *energy follows thought*. So the choices are all yours. You can use this acceleration for transformation and healing or you can give your precious energy to a dying past.

Your focused imagination and intention are incredibly powerful.

> **Abundance**
>
> AFFIRMATION: *All my needs are met above and beyond my greatest expectations.*
>
> *Open yourself to receive. Avalanches of abundance are waiting to flood your being. Everything is blossoming and bearing fruit now! The prosperity you seek is yours.*

How can you take advantage of this important time? How can you make it work in your own life? Denise Linn advises to create a *Vision Seed Collage* for the future. Creating a collage for your desired future is a very powerful Soul Coaching tool. It gives form to the unseen and there are so many transformational ways to do collages. In other words, it's an opportunity to receive what you wish to attract into your life.

When creating a collage, choose all the pictures you like from magazines, including words and phrases that match the desires you wish to manifest in your life. Trust your intuition and follow your heart. You don't need to be perfect. Leave space for the inspiration to come in, so spirit can guide you.

For example when I created a *Vision Seed Map* for a journey to Hawaii, I started to choose pictures and words that gave me the feeling of harmony, joy, balance and beauty. Getting in touch with the 'feelings' that you want to experience as a result of attaining your desires is one of the keys for a successful manifestation. To intensify these 'feelings,' do a Soul Journey and imagine that you have already reached your goals. This is very important! Then place your collage in a place where its energy can be absorbed by your subconscious. From first-hand experience I can say that every time I looked at my 'Aloha Collage' a flush of joy, a wave of energy filled my whole being. As a result, it immediately influenced my body – my body language changed into the direction of balance and harmony.

During the following weeks I came across CDs with Hawaiian music and DVDs about the Hawaiian Islands. These further deepened my 'Aloha Feelings.' It seemed as if the universe was composing something, and I always felt grateful for this. Then suddenly I got a special offer for a trip to Hawaii, an offer we could afford. Unfortunately the actual dates didn't match my husband's scheduled activities. Instead of being unhappy we accepted this and guess what happened? This offer led us to an even better one which was absolutely perfect! So hold on to your dreams. They are coming! Keep in your mind that the universe is unfolding and orchestrating your dreams and desires in many wondrous ways. Acceptance and gratitude are important keys.

On returning back from Hawaii I created an 'Aloha Corner' in our home: a small table where I placed things I had collected in Hawaii. In my opinion it is not important what you put on your table; it is the meaning you give these things. Whenever I am at home and look at this table, it's easier for me to reconnect with the feeling of joy and harmony I once experienced on the Hawaiian Islands. Creating a center in your home where you can relax, regenerate and find balance might be helpful for you, too. Feel free to try this.

Let me share with you a story about Richard. I met Richard in Taos Pueblo, New Mexico some years ago. "Call me Richard!" He told me in perfect German, when he heard me speaking German with my husband. I looked at him and there he was standing in front of me, an old man with a magical twinkle in his eyes and with a black World War II Veteran cap on his head. Richard told me that he was born in Taos Pueblo. As a little boy he always wanted to get to know the world outside the pueblo. So as a young man he joined the army and spent many years in Europe, then after World War II, several years in Heidelberg, Germany.

In his older days he returned to Taos Pueblo and guess what happened! Richard was very excited when he explained this. "As a young man I left home to see more of the world. Now in my old days the world comes to me. So many tourists from all over the world visit Taos Pueblo every day! People from Japan, Italy, Canada, Australia, France, Germany, South America . . . I am so grateful for this! I enjoy every day!" Richard gave us a big hug when we said good-bye. His awareness and humility touched my heart! I felt that the universe was whispering to me:

You are a creator and things just happen. It's a dance! One of the big keys is not to get too attached to the outcome. Accept and embrace everything as it is. Focus on what you are grateful for and enjoy your life!

Staying in Abundance Consciousness

Here is a simple exercise that I have found very effective for staying in abundance consciousness. Practice it for at least 10 to 15 minutes a day.

It is so simple that you can easily integrate it into your daily routine. You can even walk around; you don't have to sit in a yoga position.

Notice and acknowledge abundance all around you, wherever you may be. For example when you are at home, notice and acknowledge the abundance of glasses in your cupboard, the abundance of plates in your kitchen, the abundance of books in your bookshelves, the abundance of dust on the books etc. and be grateful for it. How long can you stay in an abundance consciousness until your mind takes over again and thinks about other things? When this happens, be grateful again. Say to yourself: "OK. No problem. Let's acknowledge abundance again!"

Integrate this simple practice into your daily life. After a while you will have more peace of mind; inspiration can come in more easily and you will discover more opportunities!

The most beautiful thing about this practice is that you are also training yourself to stay in the present moment. It is a most welcome side-effect. The awareness of abundance connects you with the present moment. In the present moment you are free from the control of your mind and you become connected with the truth of your soul.

Your soul loves the truth.

Every time you practice an exercise in abundance consciousness or undertake a *Soul-Journey* – don't forget to drink water! Remember that your body mostly consists of water. Unfortunately many people don't drink enough water! If your cells are dehydrated how can you live abundance in your life? So a good simple thing to do is to drink a lot of water during your day – be nice to your cells. Before you start drinking the water you can think the words *abundance* and *gratitude* – you can even write these words on your glass!

Denise Linn tells in her book *Unlock the Secret Messages Of Your Body*: "There is a life-force field that's within us and around us and our body isn't separate from that field." In other words we are living in an ocean of energy and we are all part of the abundance of vibrations of the *field*.

Try this guided meditation to increase your vitality and maybe your health. It's a good idea to do it in a natural environment so you easily access the healing forces nature is offering.

Take a few deep breaths and relax. Know that all is well. Relax and let go. There is a place beneath the surface that is still and serene; a place that knows all is well. Sink into that place. Breathe and relax.

Visualize your body as a vessel. Let sparkling silver light from the earth flow up through you . . . through your feet, knees, legs, hips, pelvis, spine, arms, neck, head . . . through your whole body. Take time to visualize. Breathe and let go!

Then imagine a sparkling golden light from heaven cascading down upon you. Through your head, spine, arms, pelvis, hips, legs, knees, feet. Breathe in and breathe out. Relax! Let go!

Imagine your cells opening up to this sparkling silver and golden life-force energy. Take time to visualize yourself merging with this life-force energy and imagine your cells absorbing energy from the universe.

Know this: Your imagination in a focused way is very powerful. Breathe!

Let a warmth grow inside of you. Take time to feel it deeply and fully! Let go!

Let your body express itself with a spontaneous humming! Good! Allow it to increase! Allow it to flow through you. All is well!

Breathe and imagine every cell in your body radiating with love – with unconditional love!

Enjoy this feeling of peace and well-being!

Feel yourself being in a place of love and unity with all things. Rest in it! Relax. That's who you are. That's where you come from. Breathe. There is nothing to do – just be. Relax! This is home. Enjoy! Take your time! Breathe deeply and fully!

After a while count to ten. Slowly and gently open your eyes.

Stretching now . . . and grounding.

During your day, love and honor your body for being such a glorious portal for the abundance of energy the universe is offering us. Give thanks for this!

Bibliography

Linn, Denise. *Soul Coaching.* Hay House, 2003

Linn, Denise. *The Secrete Language of Signs.* Ballantine Books, 1996

Linn, Denise. *The Soul Loves The Truth.* Hay House, 2006

Linn, Denise. *Mumblings & Musings Newsletter, January* 2010. www.deniselinn.com

Linn, Denise. *Unlock The Secret Messages Of Your Body.* Hay House 2010

Audios

Linn, Denise. *Soul Coaching.* Hay House Radio, Show Archives.

Further Reading

Braden, Gregg. *Secrets of the Lost Mode of Prayer.* Hay House 2006

Tolle, Eckhart. *A New Earth: Awakening to Your Life's Purpose.* Dutton 2005

Linn, Denise. *Past Lives, Present Miracles.* Hay House 2008

MacGregor, Catriona. *Partnering With Nature.* Atria Paperback 2010

Gratitude

AFFIRMATION: This is a glorious time
to be alive, and I am so grateful!

The universe is grateful for you!
Appreciation for everything flows
through you in great bounty. Cherish
the preciousness of life and everyone
and everything around you.

JUDY WARD
Kingston, Ontario, Canada

JUDY WARD has been pursuing her own journey of spiritual growth and emotional healing for many years. She currently teaches many different forms of holistic healing, spiritual growth and energy work at local community colleges and independently through her holistic teaching and treatment practice called "Search for Spirit." Judy has trained with many of the world's recognized leaders in holistic, spiritual and emotional health and brings this knowledge and learning to her practice. She has a passion for sharing and teaching and always treats her clients and students with compassion and understanding.

Judy is certified in Usui Reiki, Karuna Reiki, Integrated Energy Therapy and is an Angel Therapy Practitioner®, Certified by Doreen Virtue. She is a Certified Counselling Hypnotist and Past Life Regressionist as well as a Certified Teacher of Adults. Judy is a lifelong learner who is passionate about teaching, animals, hiking and reading uplifting books. She became a Soul Coach, Certified by Denise Linn in May of 2009.

Judy now lives in a small village just outside of Kingston, Ontario, Canada called Battersea. For consultations, readings, treatments or workshops contact Judy at judy.ward@sympatico.ca or check out her website at www.SearchforSpirit.ca

Life is a Smorgasbord of Choices!

JUDY WARD

If we let our creativity flow we discover that there are
hundreds of choices, just like a Smorgasbord.

As I stand in front of a Smorgasbord, I see a vast array of tables filled with scrumptious foods that all look, taste and smell wonderful. The vibrant and varied colors, textures and aromas are a delight and a feast for my senses! Standing before them with my plate in my hand, I contemplate the many choices I have to make. There is not enough room for everything and so I must decide what I will choose to eat. As I walk from table to table, new smells and sights enchant my senses. The choices vary, from tables of healthy fruits and vegetables to a variety of colorful salads and choices of meats, pastas, eggs and seafood. Last but not least, there are those scrumptious tables filled with delicious, creamy desserts. Choice upon choice must be made!

Of course, like everyone else, I overfill my plate with different tastes, flavors and smells. And I try to eat them all, only to return with another plate to the dessert table, where I choose to enjoy several of those rich, delightful chocolate, creamy and fattening desserts. I keep eating until I am so full that I'm uncomfortable and can barely walk out of the room. I seem to lose all sense of balance about what is good for me, or enough for me and what is good for my digestive system and for my health. I often choose things that I know are not good for me. I justify this by saying, "Oh well, I paid for them and they are there, so why not enjoy them? I deserve this."

I'm sure that you can relate to this experience, since life can be just like that Smorgasbord. There are so many choices as to what we do and don't want to experience. There are things that are good for us and there are things that are not so good for us. It really is up to us to choose what we fill our lives with. We can choose positive experiences or live in the shadow of our negative experiences. Many people say "Well, this is just happening to me and I didn't choose it." That may be true, but you always have the choice to move out of one experience and into something better.

The ability to choose applies not only to our physical body but also to the other three equally important aspects of our being. These include our mental aspect (our thoughts and beliefs), our emotional aspect (all of our emotions), and our spiritual aspect (where we are connected with our purpose and to something greater than ourselves). Only when the choices we make are balanced and supportive of all four of the basic components of our being can we be truly happy and live a life filled with joy. The choices we make affect this process, and once again, are up to us.

When presented with the Smorgasbord of life, we make use of our five senses to help us decide which experiences we prefer, and which ones we don't. We decide if something is good or bad for us by how it looks to us, how it sounds to us, whether it tastes or smells good or bad, or how it feels to us. When we make good choices that support who we really are and all of the aspects of our being, we begin to soar spiritually. As we honor our body which is truly the temple that houses our soul, let go of negative beliefs and thoughts that no longer support us, and learn to forgive and love, we move into a place in our lives where we can experience more joy. We learn to love life again! It's important to attend to all four aspects of our being, not just one or two. We need to feed and nurture each one of them to remain balanced and in harmony.

I once heard it said that *each person is a house with four rooms – physical, mental, emotional and spiritual – and unless we enter each room each day, we cannot be a whole and complete person.* My interpretation of this statement is that we must honor and take care of our bodies each day, acknowledge and feel all of our emotions as well as release the negative ones, be aware of and let go of negative beliefs and patterns as they surface, and connect with our spiritual self or our soul every day, in order to be a whole and happy person.

When I think about how my life has changed in recent years to a much more positive, and happy one, I realize this is because of the many choices I have made – little things I have changed, and steps I've taken to move closer to who I really am and who I wish to be. I learned that as I continued to make the same old choices and do the same things, I continuously got the same results. I needed to change. My soul was constantly telling me what it wanted and needed, but most of the time, the stress, noise and fear in my life prevented me from hearing the guidance of my soul. My life was so filled with clutter and baggage that I didn't hear the sound of my own soul trying to direct me to a better place. I had to do things the hard way. Still I did it, step by step, and change by change. I spent years after the separation from my first husband, trying to figure out who I really was. I had no real sense of my true identity. During that marriage I had been a wife, a daughter, a daughter-in-law, a sister, a mother and a career person. Everyone had expectations of me and wanted me to be something that they thought I should be, and I tried to fulfill all of their wishes. I had such a sense of responsibility for everyone – everyone that is, except myself. I allowed my wants and needs to go by the wayside. I would strive to fulfill everyone else's needs first and then if there was time left over, and if everyone thought it was okay, only then would I attend to my own needs, though my soul was crying to be heard. Amidst the overwhelming clutter of responsibilities, expectations, stress, the needs of others, and just day-to-day survival, the loving cry of my soul got lost in the shuffle.

After the separation from my first husband, I spent years on my own, discovering what I liked and didn't like, what I wanted in a new partner, how I wanted to make a living, and simply trying to heal the wounds that had been inflicted on me by myself and others. I tried many new things but if I didn't love them, I let them go. I learned that I am a gentle soul who likes nature, animals and quiet time alone. I learned that I loved to cook new things, although I seldom took the time. I loved to read, I loved yoga and I wanted to write. I chose to slow down and appreciate nature and animals. As I moved through the shifts and changes that were occurring, I learned to forgive myself for my mistakes and forgive others for hurting me. As I learned how to be gentler with myself, I knew I also wanted a gentle soul to share my life with me – one who would respect and love me, and one who would let me be who I really am and not try to change me.

Little by little, life became better and I attracted a wonderful man into my life – a soul companion who respected and liked me. It was such a surprise that we liked many of the same things! As I shifted and healed I realized that I wanted to help others heal their lives as well. In my everyday life I had often played the role of counselor and teacher to the people around me. I began teaching others what I had learned to help them begin their own sacred journey of healing and finding their own spirit. It took me years to make the necessary changes, and as I guided others, I guided myself as well on a journey of discovery. I learned what kind of music I liked, what kind of television I wanted to watch, that I loved the theatre, uplifting books, good food and hiking. I felt best outside in nature, communing with the animals, birds and trees. As I began to feed my soul what it wanted by incorporating the things I loved into my life, little by little each day, my own happiness gradually increased, even amidst life's daily challenges. And there were many challenges.

Synchronicity was at play when I attended a workshop with Sonia Choquette in Chicago. I met a woman there who had attended the Soul Coaching program with Denise Linn. I'd never heard of Denise Linn before that, but was intrigued. After reading some of her books I felt drawn to become a Certified Soul Coach.

I attended the training at Summerhill Ranch as a teacher, expecting to get information on how to support others in this program, only to discover that it changed my life! Healing took place at a very deep level, a level that I'd never been able to reach before, and once again I was able to make major shifts in a new direction. I knew absolutely what I wanted to do. I discovered that Soul Coaching has the magical quality of being able to shorten many years of growth and healing down to just 28 days.

I became very excited about leading others on this amazing journey of self discovery, of facing the truth about where they were in their lives and discovering how to move forward into a more positive place. I've seen amazing healing take place among the women who've taken my Soul Coaching program, in an incredibly short time. This program has now become a major part of my teaching practice. The 28 days of Soul Coaching involves a complete clearing of that inner clutter which consists of old negative thoughts, beliefs and emotions that keep us stuck in feeling bad about ourselves. This allows us to move into gratitude and happiness. It is also about clearing the outer clutter in our lives which gives us a sense of freedom and makes space for new energy and new experiences to come into our lives. It empowers us to make choices that are good for us and to let go of those that are not. Every choice we make in our lives, even the little ones, either moves us closer to who we really are and to true happiness and joy, or away from it.

The Soul Coaching program is based on working with the four aspects of self – physical, emotional, mental and spiritual through the four elements of air, water, fire and earth. We clear away the inner and outer clutter from each of these aspects of self. It is an exercise in telling the truth to ourselves about what works in our lives and what doesn't. When we do this in a balanced way, we can begin to evolve in a natural, healthy way. We can begin to make better choices that support our true well-being.

Essence

AFFIRMATION: In my essence, I am joy.

Find your essence. Simplify and contemplate in the Zen garden of your mind. Discover the stillness in the center of the cyclone; do what's important and let go of the rest.

Once you commit to this program, amazing things begin to happen in your life, as synchronicities occur and healing begins, sometimes at such a deep level that often we aren't even aware of it. But nevertheless, it is happening. And life is never the same again. As you move through the 28 days of the group program, you experience many 'Ah Ha' moments and can begin to make choices that move you closer to your authentic self. You will change or let go of some habits and behaviors that no longer serve you. You can truly let them go because you realize you don't need them anymore. And you become soul sisters or brothers with the other members of your group as you support each other through the journey. Lifelong friendships often develop during this magical four week program. Healing takes place so much more easily than it had on my own journey, which had taken years.

Many of us do not take good care of our physical body, represented by the element of earth. Through Soul Coaching I became more aware of those times when I was filling my body with junk foods and unhealthy substances. I was able to notice how different I felt when I didn't exercise or stretch my body. I no longer looked in the mirror with disgust at what I saw, but started to see the amazing temple that houses my soul. A temple is a holy place that must be honored and respected. It needs to be cared for and nurtured in a loving way. When I started to think of my body as the temple that houses my soul, I realized that my body needs nurturing as well. And when I began to make choices that supported my physical body, my body responded.

I started to cook and eat more nutritious meals and cut down on sweets, alcohol and caffeine. I started to walk outside and breathe in deeply the clean, fresh air, and when my body was tired, I allowed it to rest. I started to listen to the messages of my body and joined a yoga class. My body told me when it was tired and needed to relax or rest. In the past when I had felt pain I would just take a pill and say "Shut up body, I don't have time for this." Now I know this means I need to change one of my behaviors instead. I seldom take any form of drug these days, unless absolutely necessary. My body tells me which foods make me feel sluggish or heavy and which ones give me energy. I now listen more closely to these messages from my physical self and no longer choose to ignore them.

As I connect more deeply with mother earth and the animals by walking my dog in nature (which always seeks harmony), I now have a real awareness that we humans are also a part of nature. I have regained my own natural rhythm which had been lost in the busy days of life. Soul Coaching has enabled me to slow down and make even better choices to support my body. Yet I know that regaining a sense of balance in the physical body is only one part of the process.

The emotional side of our being, represented by the element of water, is all about how we feel. It contains all of our emotions, not just the ones we are currently experiencing, but all the emotions we have ever felt in our life. This aspect of self contains all of our loves and our capacity for happiness, compassion and forgiveness. It also contains our darker shadow emotions like anger, fear, jealousy, resentment, hopelessness and disgust. It is well known that suppressing negative emotions can cause us to lose energy and to become exhausted, often driving us into depression.

I began to use my emotions as a compass to point me in the direction I wished to move. When I felt happy or peaceful, which are the highest vibrations possible for us to feel, I knew I was on the right path to who I really am. Life became fun and it felt good! When I was stuck in anger, jealousy, or fear, the lowest vibrational feelings we can feel, I knew I was off the path to who I really am. Life was not fun! And so I strove to remain more positive and to focus on feeling grateful for what was good in my life.

At first I blamed others for their mistreatment of me and didn't know how to forgive them, and wasn't even sure if I wanted to. I had been stuck in fear and anger long enough to know that I always felt drained when I felt such emotions. Bad things happen to people all the time and by staying stuck in fear or anger, it only hurts you, by storing that toxic energy in your body. I didn't want to carry that heavy toxic energy any more. Once I was willing to forgive myself and others,

I was finally able to move forward into a new and better life. Using my emotions as a compass to guide me, I regularly ask myself "How do I feel right now – do I feel good or do I feel bad?" If I feel angry, bitter, jealous, or fearful, I try to let that go and to think about something good in my life. I shift my energy towards something more positive. When we become aware of our negative emotions we can make a conscious decision to stay in our positive energy more often, and truly begin to create the more positive life we really want.

The third aspect of our being is the mental component, represented by the element of air. I often teach that a belief is only a thought that has been thought over and over until we believe it, or something we have been told over and over again until we believe it. Often our beliefs have been taught to us by people of authority when we were children (such as parents, teachers or even friends who we thought were more powerful than us). They sometimes told us negative things, and we believed them, and often, at a deep subconscious level, they became our beliefs. But they aren't always true! Remember that just because man once believed that the earth was flat doesn't mean it was true. And so I took a look at some of my old beliefs such as "I must never be dependent on or trust any man," and "I'm not good enough." I came to understand that these things are not true.

So as I shifted my thoughts and let go of old beliefs that were not true and did not serve me, my life shifted again and again. We can discover our negative beliefs by listening to the way we talk to ourselves. I would say things like, "How could I be so stupid?" or "Men can't be trusted – I don't want to get hurt again." When I heard myself say "I'd rather be alone," I felt the untruth of this statement at a core level and knew that it was fear talking. I learned that I didn't want or need these old beliefs and have let them go, one by one, and have replaced them with more positive and life-affirming beliefs.

The fourth aspect of our being is the spiritual component, represented by the element of fire. This is where we gain access to universal guidance, where we develop our passion for life, and where we can discover our real purpose for being here. The soul knows the truth about who we are, and as I started to tell the truth about my life, the good and the bad and the ugly, my soul helped me to face my fears and discover who I really am and what I truly want. As I cleared away the inner and outer clutter of my life, my soul spoke to me and I began to discover my true purpose in life. And when I truly connected with my spiritual self, I felt a sense of peace and joy that I had never experienced before.

It seems that when our physical, emotional and mental aspects are in balance we turn naturally to our spiritual self. However, this is not always the case. Sometimes it is our spiritual nature that helps us to balance the other aspects of self. As I began to listen to the wisdom of my own soul, I was able to move into a state of balance and a new way of being. I again made different and better choices. I realized that all life is about spiritual growth. We have come here with a purpose: to serve, to share, to experience, to find joy and happiness, to love and to grow spiritually. Our choices can help us do that. When we make choices that make us happy, we *feed our soul*.

Soul Coaching can help us clarify what we want to let go of and what is valuable in our lives. This program is about telling yourself the truth about your life, facing your deepest fears and challenges and recognizing the love that you are. As you clear away the clutter that conceals the real you, you can make choices, large and small, that resonate at a deep level and feed your soul. As you complete the inner and outer clearing through this program, you will clearly hear the guidance from your soul. You will discover what you truly love and what makes you happy. Soul Coaching enables us to take back our power and make positive choices so that we can live a balanced life filled with joy, love, compassion, forgiveness and self love. This is a program you can do time and time again. Each time I do the 28 day program myself, I see how much more I have grown. And I am happy knowing that my life will never be the same again.

Every day is a chance to begin again and to make different choices, just as in the Smorgasbord. As we listen to the murmurings of our soul trying to get our attention amidst the chaos, fear, stress and anger, we can begin to make choices (even small ones) that support our well-being. Our soul needs to be fed and nurtured and we need to start noticing those little moments of joy that happen each day. We each have them. Each person is different and so, like the Smorgasbord, you need to decide what choices you will make. What feeds your soul? What do you love? What makes you happy? If you let your creativity flow and enjoy the process, you will discover that there are hundreds of choices, just like at a Smorgasbord. What will you choose to feed yourself today?

What are Your Energy Zappers and Juicers?

In your life there are people, places, things and experiences that uplift you and make you feel good, or juice your energy, and there are those that zap your energy or drag you down. An energy zapper is anything that lowers your energy level, or makes you feel bad, or puts you in a negative mood.

Here's a simple exercise that I have found very effective. In a journal or on a piece of paper, create two lists: one called *Things that Juice my Energy* and one called *Things that Zap my Energy*. Over the course of a whole day, notice how you feel with every person, experience or object that you encounter and add them to one of your lists.

At the end of the day, review your *Things that Juice your Energy* List. Feel how good these people, places, things or experiences make you feel. For example: It feels so good when I go for a walk with my dog in the park where it is peaceful and I can connect with nature. Or it feels so good to visit and play with my grandchildren. Another might be: It feels good to soak in a hot bubble bath with a good book. Choose two of the things that juice your energy, and plan to increase the time you spend on these energy juicers over the next week.

Next, review your *Things that Zap my Energy* List. Feel how tired they make you feel or how they drag your energy down to a lower level. Examples might be: every time you look at that lamp that Aunt Sally gave you, you realize how much you dislike it. You only keep it just in case she visits. Get rid of it! Or, every time you look at a certain object, it reminds you of the painful breakup of a relationship. Get it out of your home! Let it go and move forward into your new life without that reminder of the painful past. Clutter can also be an energy zapper, so get rid of those old newspapers or magazines that you know you won't read and simply represent stagnant energy in your home. It is a real energy juicer to do clutter clearing in your home or car. Make a choice to eliminate one or two zappers from your list. As you complete these tasks over the next week, notice the increase in your energy level.

As you see and feel the effects of reducing those energy zappers, continue letting go of or at least reducing the time spent with those energy zappers. Continue to increase those energy juicers!

Just like a smorgasbord, the choices are all yours! Why not chose a magnificent, happy life!

Simplicity

AFFIRMATION: Deep, profound serenity is expanding my life!

Do what matters; and release the rest to find peace, grace, and stillness. Clear internal and external clutter.

ILONA WARDA
Mississauga, Ontario, Canada

ILONA WARDA is a Registered Holistic Practitioner, Yoga Instructor, Certified Soul Coach and Past Life Coach. She has been on a spiritual path for many years and has a passion to assist others on their journey of healing, transformation and self-discovery. Ilona was born in Poland and is currently living in Mississauga, Ontario, Canada. She has had the honor of training with many wonderful and inspirational teachers such as Denise Linn, founder of Soul Coaching, Drs. Deepak Chopra and David Simon, founders of The Chopra Center for Well-Being, all of whom are changing the world by expanding awareness in the area of physical, emotional, mental and spiritual health. She is committed to following the same path.

Her dream came true when she was able to create the Holistic Yoga and Meditation Center. Ilona facilitates workshops and seminars for personal-growth, practices Holistic Healing including Reiki and teaches Yoga and Meditation classes. Her mission is to help each person on a physical, emotional, mental and spiritual level by offering the many different modalities available at her Center. She is currently expanding her dream to create Holistic Yoga Teachers' Training. She wishes to share her passion and knowledge with all who are on a similar path and are interested in becoming professional Holistic Yoga Instructors.

For workshops, seminars, classes, healing and teachers' training, contact Ilona at ilonawarda@yahoo.ca or www.GoHolisticYoga.ca

Turning Points

ILONA WARDA

Yoga, Meditation and Soul Coaching all work very well together,
because Soul Coaching is about aligning our
inner spiritual life with our outer life.

A turning point can be a time when you make an empowering or dis-empowering decision that affects your life from that moment onward. When you become aware of these important moments, you will gain more understanding of why you have made certain decisions about your life and yourself. Most likely, some of these meaningful events still affect your life in a positive or negative way. When you are willing to stop judging your experiences and accept them as part of your growth, you are able to find some positive lessons from these experiences.

Everyone experiences some challenging moments at some point in his or her life, but what is important is the way our mind deals with these challenges. You have the power to choose the empowering meaning for each event, even the most difficult one. Sometimes you may not understand why you had to go through these difficult moments, but if you keep your mind open and listen to the whispers of your soul, you may discover the lessons from the experiences.

If you are blaming something or somebody for what has happened in your life, you will feel you have no control over your life and you will lose the power to change your situation. When you are able to release the victim thinking, you will start to feel you are in charge of your life. No matter what happened on your journey, with each breath you take, you have a new chance to transform your life. Everything happens for a reason, and acceptance without judgment allows us to understand those reasons. There is a beautiful Zen Story I would like to share with you. This story clearly illustrates the folly of making judgments, the practice of acceptance and the meaning we give to each experience.

A long time ago in a small farming village there lived a farmer and his son. This farmer was widowed and very poor. He owned a horse and a small piece of land. The father and son worked their little piece of land to support themselves and lived a simple, happy life. Every morning the farmer woke at dawn and stepped outside his little dwelling to greet the sun. He would stand, taking in the sun's rays and thanking the creator for its beauty and wonder.

One morning he arose as usual to perform his morning ritual before waking his son to share a simple breakfast together. He then went to feed his horse. When he arrived at his paddock, he found several men from the village standing around his gate. The gate was broken and there was no sign of his horse. 'You poor man,' they said. 'Your only horse has run off into the mountains. How will you plough your fields now? You must have done something very bad to invoke the gods' fury in this way; they must be very angry with you.' The farmer replied, 'perhaps.'

Next morning the farmer arose as usual and after breakfast went to his paddock to repair his broken gate. As he arrived, he found the same group of men in his paddock. There, standing in the paddock, was the farmer's horse with six wild horses. 'You must be the luckiest man alive,' they said. 'Your horse has returned and brought six other horses with it. You are rich! The gods must be smiling on you today.' The farmer replied, 'perhaps'.

Next day, the farmer's son arose and began to break in one of the wild horses. However, when he climbed onto its back he was thrown off. As he hit the ground, he broke one of his legs. The villagers now said, 'you poor man. For the next six weeks, your son will not be able to work. You will have to tend your crops alone. You must be the unluckiest man alive.' The farmer said, 'perhaps.'

Before dawn the next morning, the farmer woke up to a loud commotion. He saw many soldiers in the village when he stepped outside. The village men said, 'We are doomed. The emperor has brought our country to war and all the healthy, young men are being taken away to fight. You are so lucky that your son's leg is broken. His leg will soon heal, but many of our sons may never return from this war. The gods must surely favor you.' The farmer replied, 'perhaps.'

This story illustrates that we never really know whether something that occurs is good or bad. Similarly, what appears good can sometimes turn out to be bad.

Sometimes it is not easy to recognize our life patterns on our own; that is why I would like to recommend the profound Soul Coaching Program created by Denise Linn.

Soul Coaching takes us on a wonderful journey of self-discovery and transformation. It is a process that guides you to connect with your inner self, helping you to find meaning and sacredness in your everyday life. You will be guided as you take an honest look at yourself, your life, face fear, release old negative patterns, get motivated, and step joyfully into your future! The Soul Coaching Program is divided into four weeks, with each week representing an element of nature. Each element corresponds to an aspect of Self. Air – represents our mental body, Water – our emotional body, Fire – spiritual body, and Earth – our physical body. Connecting with each element brings profound changes in our lives. Because the Water element is connected with our emotional body, one of the activities in water week is to explore our turning points in life and the emotional meaning we give to our experiences. This week may trigger some emotional cleansing but this is part of the process.

For me, examining my turning points was an eye-opening experience! There were times when I also questioned myself, why I had to go through so many challenges in my life. However, when I realized that everything was part of my growth I felt so much better.

I used to describe my childhood as challenging; I felt this way because of my Dad's behavior. When he came home drunk, he would become very aggressive and abusive towards my Mom and us-children. Sometimes we had to leave our home just to avoid harm. I did not feel safe. There was always fear, and no peace in my home. At the age of only six years old, I made my decision never to be like my dad. I did not want to have any habits like him: aggressiveness, violence, drinking, smoking or swearing.

> *Your living is determined not so much by what life brings to you*
> *as by the attitude you bring to life, not so much by what happens to you*
> *as by the way your mind looks at what happens.*

−KAHLIL GIBRAN

After exploring this turning point in my life, I made a conscious choice to learn from my challenges and empower myself rather than disempower myself. By seeing this life challenge from a place of empowerment, I can see that my father actually helped me to make a decision to live a healthy lifestyle from a very young age. This decision has led me on a life-long path towards health and happiness in every aspect of my life.

Another turning point in my life was my divorce. It took a long time to get to the point when I realized that my marriage was not working. My husband and I tried many times to make it work, but somehow we could not succeed. There were issues that we were unable to resolve. Making the decision to live on my own was very challenging. I had no place to go, no money and no steady job. I was afraid to be on my own, but the only thing I truly desired was peace. However, I did have one essential ingredient that sustained me – I had faith and trust that everything would work out, and . . . it did!

Slowly, I started to change my life. I learned how to survive on my own and take responsibility for myself. I noticed each time I was presented with a challenge to overcome, I became stronger, more confident and, in the process, learned to trust myself more. Looking back now, I can see clearly the lessons I had to learn. I needed to learn to be independent, responsible, creative, and have the determination to follow my dream. I am thankful now for all the opportunities that came to my life to help me grow more. We give meaning to each situation in our life.

We can choose something that will empower us and give us strength to create the life we want. It is good to remember the law of energy: *where our intention goes the energy flows.* We have to make sure we focus in the right direction! *We need to avoid the 'victim' role because as soon as we become the victim, we lose the power to change our lives.*

I will share one more turning point from my own life with the intention to inspire you. Even when you are faced with a health challenge, don't give up; you can use this as your learning process to change your life. When I was diagnosed with an under-active thyroid, my doctor said there was no cure for this condition, so I would have to take pills for the rest of my life. Since I never take any pills, I decided to do some research and found out that the medicine had many side effects. I was always interested in alternative medicine and so decided to explore a natural approach to heal my thyroid while I was taking the pills. One of my friends contacted me with a referral to a great energy healer. I had some healing sessions with him, than stopped my medication for one month. Then I decided to have my thyroid rechecked. When I went back to my doctor and underwent a series of tests, all my results showed that my thyroid was now functioning normally. I was amazed!

I wanted to learn everything from this amazing healer, so I attended all the courses and workshops he offered. I had discovered my passion! I wanted to learn all there was to know about energy healing. I learned a lot from him and then decided to go further by studying Reiki, Therapeutic Touch, Chakra Balancing, Trigger Point Massage and Ear Candling. I discovered my path; I knew that this is what I wanted to do with my life. And, I became a Registered Holistic Practitioner and I started my practice.

That was just beginning. My path unfolded day by day. I began looking for a yoga center where I could focus on my Body, Mind and Spirit. I found a good place and started to practice yoga and meditation. After committing myself to unlimited classes and all of the workshops they offered, I experienced profound changes within myself and in my life. I began to have a clear vision of what I would like to create in my life. Yoga, Meditation and Holistic Healing became my passion.

My dream was to create a sacred place where all of these modalities could be brought together. I went deeper into my practice and became a Yoga Instructor. But I did not stop there. I opened my own Holistic Yoga and Meditation Center in Mississauga, Ontario. Incorporating Yoga, Meditation and Holistic Healing helped me to create a sacred place where the focus is on all the levels of our existence. In each of our yoga classes, we address all aspects of Self, working on our physical, mental, emotional and spiritual bodies. Going through each aspect of our Self creates a healthy body, positive attitude, peace, harmony and emotional stability.

To complement the classes and programs we offer, I also became a Soul Coach certified by Denise Linn. Yoga, Meditation and Soul Coaching all work very well together, because Soul Coaching is about aligning our inner spiritual life with our outer life. It helps us to clear away mental, emotional, spiritual and physical clutter so that we can hear the messages from within. Yoga practice also focuses on clearing the clutter from our mental, emotional, spiritual and physical body so we can connect with our True Self, and expand our awareness. I realized that getting sick was one of the most powerful turning points of my life because it allowed me to find my true purpose and passion in life.

I encourage you to find positive aspects of your own turning points and use this to empower yourself and take action to fulfill your dreams. That is what the Soul Coaching Program challenges us to do. We cannot change some of the events that happen in our lives, but we can change our approach and the meaning we give to them. The Soul Coaching Program asks us to clear the clutter from our lives, both from the inside (within our body) and outside (within our environment). It urges us to allow our soul to lead us in living the most fulfilling life possible.

Whenever I facilitate the Soul Coaching Program, my heart fills with joy when I see so many changes, transformation and healing taking place for participants attending the workshop. Let me share one of our participant's stories about taking the Soul Coaching Program and her life changing experience.

Vanessa came to the Center for assistance when she became tired of fighting with her own mind, unable to get the answers she was seeking. Overwhelmed by her emotions, she was experiencing anxiety, depression and severe confusion. Although she had tried many different methods to relieve her condition, including medication, nothing had worked. Vanessa was willing to do anything she could to improve her state of mind, her health and the quality of her life.

> ### Transformation
>
> *AFFIRMATION: I am joyously centered and safe as wonderful changes occur around me!*
>
> *Positive changes are coming. Old structures, beliefs and ideas are falling away and will be replaced with vitality and new pathways. Soon you'll be seeing the world in a fresh way.*

When Vanessa and her husband first dropped by, she looked emotionally exhausted and my heart went out to her. I really wanted to help. She shared honestly with me some of the troubling issues she was experiencing and that she felt she had nothing to lose by trying something new. Since she was willing to try yoga and meditation, I recommended that she attend classes regularly to make her body stronger and help her to quiet down her mind.

Vanessa began to show signs of improvement as she began her regular yoga practice, although she still needed to release the emotions that she had been storing in her body for many years. She was very sincere about attending all of our classes and workshops designed to release these blockages, and had begun to feel much better; but she was still struggling with quieting down her mind. She had many questions and had been looking for the answers outside of herself. I felt that Vanessa needed something more and was ready to take the next step.

I will never forget the look in her eyes when she asked with disbelief, "Are you telling me that I will be able to quiet down my mind, to actually relax my mind?" "Yes you will," I said. Vanessa just laughed. The next important step in her healing was to attend the Soul Coaching Program.

The transformation Vanessa experienced through Soul Coaching was incredible. She gave one hundred percent because she was willing to do anything to experience a peaceful mind.

At the end of Air Week, Vanessa chose the 'Pleasure' card from Denise Linn's *Soul Coaching Oracle Cards* and told me she was planning a trip to Florida with her family. She cleared a lot of her emotional clutter while on vacation in Florida and when she came back, we scheduled her in for a private session so that she could talk about her experiences from Water week. She admitted that Water week had been the most powerful turning point in her life, due to the intense emotional cleansing she had experienced.

Then we began a meditation to connect with the fire element, representing our Spiritual Self. After clearing the clutter from her mental and emotional body, she was able to connect with her spirit. This session changed her life forever. Vanessa said that she felt reborn. In her meditation, she experienced the peace, silence and nothingness that she had been trying so hard and for so long to attain. Everything became much clearer; she felt she had found answers to all of her questions. She was able to connect with her inner wisdom where she discovered that all her answers were within. Her anxiety, depression and confusion were gone.

Now there is a smile on her face and she is glowing with light. She spreads this light to her family and to all the people around her. Vanessa allowed me to share her story with you because she wants to inspire others and to give them hope. She believes that taking the Soul Coaching Program was the best choice she has ever made in her life.

These are Vanessa's reflections on her experience with Soul Coaching: "Taking the Soul Coaching Program was the greatest gift that I could give to myself. As a result, I feel free, peaceful and happy beyond reason and I am in complete harmony with my true needs. I have learned to live life moment by moment, to feel strong and be always aware of the yearnings within my soul. This amazing journey through the elements of nature helped me to connect with my heart, with my inner wisdom, allowing me to see and feel the world with love and total acceptance. I am so grateful for this life-changing experience. I find myself now in a place of gratitude, self-knowledge, and a place where acceptance and love is all there is. My attitude towards life has changed forever."

This is one of many inspiring stories. My hope is that my sharing of Vanessa's turning points and the turning points from my own life will bring you the inspiration you need, to look at your past in a different way, to accept the events and to find something that will empower and motivate you to create the life of your dreams. Now is the time to take action. No matter what has happened in your life, everything was necessary to bring you to where you are now. Celebrate your life!

It is an honor to share my personal experience. I feel very blessed to have been able to explore my journey with so many wonderful people who are traveling along a similar path. It is a journey of discovery and transformation. Not only have I experienced profound personal changes in my own life, but I have also had the pleasure of facilitating this journey for others. I am grateful to Denise Linn, founder of Soul Coaching, for giving Soul Coaches around the world the opportunity to share it with their clients and to observe the enormous difference it has made in so many lives!

Connecting with Four Elements through Yoga Postures

The four elements create the foundation of life on our planet. Each element reflects different aspect of us. We are part of nature and nature is part of us: it has a profound effect on our lives. As we become more aware of the importance of the elements, we bring more balance and harmony into our lives.

Through my practice of teaching Yoga along with the Soul Coaching Program for some time, I have noticed how well they complement each other, bringing incredible results for the participants. Through postures, breathing, relaxation and meditation we work on all four aspects of self, creating harmony, peace, positive attitude and bringing empowering energy into our lives. Described below are some yoga postures, which will help you to connect with each element.

Air Element

Be aware of your breathing. Air represents our mental body and ability to see clearly into your life and yourself. By inviting the element of Air, you will experience more acceptance, love, patience, compassion and a more positive attitude.

Cobra position – Lie face down on a mat. Extend your legs behind you. Place your hands on the floor, next to the ears, fingers pointing forward, and elbows pointing backward. As you inhale, raise your upper body; press your hips into the floor, arching your back, keeping your elbows slightly bent and close to your body and your shoulders down. Hold this position as long as it is comfortable. Breathe deeply, expanding your chest. As you exhale, lower your chest to the floor.

Water Element

Be aware of the water inside of you and outside. Water represents your emotional body and symbolizes opening and emotional cleansing. By inviting the element of Water, you can release old negative emotions and make room for positive feelings to come into your life.

Butterfly Position – Lie down on your back; bend your knees; keep your feet hip-width apart and pulled back toward your buttocks. Bring the soles of your feet together and open your knees outside like a butterfly, stay in this position for a few moments, then bring your knees together as you exhale. When your knees touch, inhale and open them again. You can do this several times.

Fire Element

Be aware of fire and light. Fire represents our spiritual body, purification and transformation. By inviting the spirit of Fire, you bring more clarity into your life, allowing you to live in the present moment.

Stomach crunches – Lie on your back with your knees bent, your feet parallel, hip-width apart. Cradle the back of your head with your palms and keep looking at the ceiling. Press your lower back down, slightly tilting your pelvis upward. Using your abdominal muscles, lift your shoulders up from the floor and hold the position for as long as it is comfortable, then slowly come back down. Exhale as you lift; inhale on the way down.

Earth Element

Be aware of any contact with the Earth. Earth represents your physical body and connection with nature. By inviting the spirit of Earth, you will feel more balanced and grounded.

Sitting in crossed-legged position – Center yourself, keeping your spine straight but relaxed. Focus on the base of your spine and imagine roots growing down into the earth, making a firm base for your trunk. You are grounded and balanced. Feel the connection and the heartbeat of the Earth. Become one with the Earth.

Believe

*AFFIRMATION: The best
is yet to come!*

*Believe in yourself!
Have faith in magic and miracles.
If you can conceive it,
you can achieve it.*

PETRA NELLA
The Netherlands and Shelburne Falls, MA, USA

WHEN PETRA WAS a young woman growing up in the Netherlands, her peers gave her the nickname "Mother Theresa." It wasn't a big surprise after graduating from high school that she became a social worker. For 5 years Petra professionally coached people who were unemployed. When she moved to the Unites States 6 years ago, Petra began working with children at a Waldorf School in Los Angeles. This helped her to reconnect with her own inner child, who loves to be creative, to be in nature, to ask questions and to live a colorful life.

After graduating from the Soul Coaching program with Denise Linn in the summer of 2009 her life changed. Petra realized that she had finally found the core of her passion by asking herself "What does your soul want you to know?"

She started her own coaching and intuitive counseling business where she combines different healing modalities such as Thought Field Therapy, Aura Soma Color Therapy, Soul Coaching, Energy Healing and working with the Angels and Masters to assist her with her counseling. Her name, Petra Nella means in Greek 'rock of light' and this is exactly what she will offer you. Petra holds wisdom like a rock and will shine her light on difficult situations, helping people to reconnect with their own light and find out what their purpose is in life. If you would like to know more you can visit her website: www.PetraNella.info

Spread Your Wings!

PETRA NELLA

When everything changes, change everything!

—NEALE DONALD WALSH

One morning at work, I was sitting at my computer, thinking about how nice it would be if I could start my own life coaching business. I found a website which allows you to design your own business cards. Then I found a nice logo of a sun with spiral rays and a turquoise background. Turquoise happens to be my favorite color. I was debating about what my title should be on the card when all of a sudden, my fingers were guided and they started typing the words *Soul Coach*. I'd heard those words somewhere before but couldn't think of where it was. That night when I went home, I was cleaning up some old paperwork and came across a brochure for Soul Coaching by Denise Linn that I'd picked up at the *I Can Do It* conference in San Diego. The next morning, I phoned the number on the brochure and Denise herself picked up. She told me that there was only one spot left for the next professional Soul Coaching training program. I just knew that this was my spot! But it had been a long journey up until this magical moment . . .

When something changes, everything changes. This is how I feel about how my life has changed since leaving my homeland, The Netherlands and my family, to get married to an American man in 2004, at the age of thirty-two. I left my life-long career with the government, including five years working as a licensed social worker. My main focus there had been to coach people who were on welfare and unemployment benefits to help them reenter the workforce. This was something I really enjoyed doing, but the bureaucratic system was preventing me from having enough time for personal contact with my clients, which I believe is very important in getting the desired results. I was slowly losing my energy and passion.

After visiting California for a two week vacation, I fell in love with a man whom I'd first met fifteen years ago. Our grandmothers were neighbors in my hometown in The Netherlands. When my mother met the mother of this man, she had invited us to visit her family in California. The first time our families met, there seemed to be too much of an age difference between us. But when I met him again, six years ago, the timing was right. After long distance dating for a year, going back and forth for short vacations in California and the Netherlands, we decided that we were ready. He had an established home and business in Los Angeles. So it seemed the logical thing to do was to leave behind my apartment, career, friends and family to be with him full time.

We really enjoyed living together for the first six months. Then, as soon as we found out that marriage was the easiest way for me to be able to have the required legal documents to stay in America and to be able to work, we decided to get married. Even though I believed this was all meant to be and that everything would work out just fine, I cannot say that we got married and lived happily ever after. The commitment of marriage had put pressure on the relationship and something shifted inside both of us, and in what we had shared together.

The first year I had not been able to work and earn any money and I felt bad that my husband was the only one providing income. I also found it hard to make friends because I didn't really know what I wanted to do in this big city, besides being with the man I loved. Everybody around me was going to work while I stayed at home. I had never experienced being a housewife and slowly became disconnected from myself. I kept asking myself "Who am I and what am I here to do?"

I felt lonely, unworthy, unsafe and not good enough. I missed my family and the support of my friends. My husband was so busy feeling responsible to provide income that he couldn't give me the emotional support I needed. When I visited The Netherlands I felt I didn't fit in there anymore either. I didn't appreciate that I lived in a beautiful area of Los Angeles, Venice Beach. I also didn't allow myself to enjoy life or take the time to find out what I really wanted to do. I could've been sitting in the sun, swimming in the ocean and watching the dolphins, pelicans and beautiful sunsets. Instead, I was beating myself up by pointing out my weaknesses and feeling sorry for myself.

On top of this, my husband felt I wasn't the same person that he fell in love with anymore, and he was right. I felt depressed and needed help; I had hit rock bottom. It was time for me to go talk to a therapist. Ironically, this step made me feel more 'normal' because who doesn't talk to a therapist in Los Angeles? In the process of getting out of this dark state, my husband joined me briefly in therapy, but decided he didn't wish to continue. He had accepted that life was good enough for him and was happy to remain in his status quo, the place that was known to him and which didn't require a lot of self-reflection and change. I felt the opposite. I wanted to grow, learn more about myself and move towards the light!

In the meantime I had started taking classes in Early Childhood Education. I didn't want to do social work with adults for the time being. I wasn't quite ready to use my social service skills; I knew I had to take care of myself first. After two semesters I was ready to work at a preschool and applied for a teaching assistant position. I can see now that working with these children really helped me to connect with my inner child again. Even though I was overqualified for this work, I found it very hard to leave this school because I had become so emotionally attached to the children. They were very grateful for the arts and crafts activities I organized for them, and showed me every day how much they loved and appreciated me with hugs, kisses and drawings. It had been a long time since I had felt being so loved. The thought of having children of my own came up and I approached the subject with my husband but it became clear that we'd grown apart. In an attempt to save the marriage we both tried to change each other. This only resulted in huge fights and eventually, we filed for divorce.

I continued going to the therapist, whom I now called 'my expensive girlfriend' while my husband and I worked through the separation process. Had this happened sooner, I might have gone back to the Netherlands after the divorce. But I had now been gone for three years and was slowly adapting to my new life and environment. I had made some friends and felt myself getting stronger each day. I also began to see that this new environment and the changes that were occurring actually provided endless opportunities for me. The love for my husband had at first seemed to be the only reason for me to leave my homeland, but I'd finally realized that I had to move away from my family in order to find my true self and to get in touch with my soul. My husband had given me this opportunity and I will always be thankful to him for that.

I now needed to find higher-paying work because I had to sustain myself alone. On the night before I said goodbye to the children at the preschool I couldn't fall asleep. I began to write, and a story came to me. It is a story about a lonely caterpillar that leaves her family to go travel and see something of the big wide world. Along the way a process of transformation begins where the caterpillar wakes up and finds herself trapped in a cocoon. She breaks free from this cocoon in order to spread her wings and fly, and she changes into a beautiful butterfly. I had never written a story before but I felt guided and moved by a higher force during this process. This is something I'd never experienced before, but it made me realize that I was protected and I no longer felt so alone.

This was the beginning of my conscious spiritual journey. Up until this point I had made most of the decisions in my life based on my thinking about what would be good for me. I had never paid much attention to my feelings. Though I've always been very creative and artistic I was afraid to express it. What would people think of me? I already felt so different. I believed that I couldn't make enough money as an artist and compared myself with my mother, who is a professional artist. I was afraid that I couldn't be as good as she is. Working with art and children had awakened a part of me that had always wanted to be an artist. But the timing wasn't yet right to do something with it.

So I found another job as the coordinator of an Early Childhood Center of a Waldorf School. The Waldorf system, founded by Rudolph Steiner, has been called "the world's best kept education secret." Its curriculum seeks to nourish a child's imagination and emotions through art and music, as well as their intellect. It was a joy working in the beautiful environment created for these children. They were made to feel safe, nurtured and free to wonder and express themselves.

It made me wish I could be a child again! This job provided stability and allowed me to develop the peace I needed. I loved being around like-minded people with a spiritual interest. In the evenings I took art classes at the Community College and proved to myself that I was indeed an artist.

I considered going back to school to obtain a Master's Degree in family and marriage counseling or art therapy. I visited a few schools but none of the programs spoke to me. A friend asked me if I wanted to join her for a workshop called 'Angel Therapy' in Sedona, Arizona. I wasn't very familiar with angels because they were not part of my upbringing. Though skeptical about the workshop, I'd heard great things about Sedona and decided to go. This trip turned out to be life-changing for me. I discovered that I could tap into divine energy and ask for help and guidance whenever I needed it.

A woman I met in the class referred me to a clairvoyant. Though I had never been to a clairvoyant before, I decided to open myself up to some new experiences in life. The clairvoyant told me that it wasn't necessary to obtain a Master's Degree in anything, but to take short programs here and there, focusing on healing and coaching. She also said that I was already prepared as a teacher and healer but needed to reconnect with the higher power, which would build up my confidence and lead to the right tools to work with. She gave me this information without me even asking about this topic. She also saw that I could be helpful for younger children, not so much as a teacher, but more by writing and telling them stories. This confirmed my butterfly story experience and made me feel both excited and scared at the same time. I wondered how I would ever be able to do this successfully if I'd never done it in my life before. But then I remembered how I felt guided when I was writing my butterfly story and just knew I had to *believe* that I could do it. From that moment on, I began to recognize more signs of confirmation that were showing up in my life.

Faith

AFFIRMATION: My life is divinely guided.

Trust that you're exactly where you need to be. Have faith in yourself and know that you're divinely guided . . . even when you have doubts. Believe! You've planted your seeds, now allow the Creator to do the rest.

Shortly after, I stumbled upon Denise Linn's brochure for Soul Coaching and knew this was a very important sign to point me in the direction I wanted to go. Soul Coaching training has provided me with the tools that I was looking for in order to start my own coaching business. I learned how to do Soul Clearing and Space Clearing using specific tools like bell clearing and feather clearing techniques. They will both clear your personal auric field and can also be used to do a space clearing in your home or work space. This usually leaves you with a very peaceful feeling afterwards. Soul journeys take you on a guided journey into the depths of your soul. You may discover you have a spirit guide, or a spirit animal, and what the meaning of this is for you. Soul Coaching also helped me to rediscover the power of the imagination.

Like many people, I must have blocked this in the process of becoming an adult by being too much in my head. In our imagination, everything is possible.

Imagination is more important than knowledge.
For knowledge is limited to all we know and understand, while imagi-
nation embraces the entire world and all there ever will be to know
and understand.

—ALBERT EINSTEIN

During my soul journey I discovered how much my soul loves to be in nature. I grew up and spent most of my life in the city, but in my new life in America I now had the opportunity to spend more time in nature. Being close to the ocean has always had a heaing effect on me.

Doing Past-life soul journeys have also been very healing for me. They have provided me with an explanation of why I had issues in my relationship with my former husband. I traveled back to several past lifetimes we had shared together. In one of them we were married. He was a soldier who had been sent overseas and died in a battle during wwii. I saw the American flag that they presented to me after his death, but remembered how I kept wondering if he had really died. This explained why I felt so happy when we found each other again in this present life. In another lifetime, I had been his mother. It now made sense to me that my former husband at times would say that I sounded like his mother. He didn't really listen to what I had to say because his relationship with his mother in this lifetime hadn't been ideal. It also became clear to me why it took so long for me to decide to separate from him. It makes the bond even stronger when you've shared so many lifetimes together with someone. It becomes difficult to let go of something that is familiar to you, even if you know that this bond is no longer healthy for either of you.

I remember pulling a Soul Coaching Oracle Card. I had asked the question: What will I gain from my commitment to Soul Coaching? When I pulled out the 'Faith' card, I remember feeling a little disappointed because I had hoped to pull the 'Abundance' card. This is such a common human reaction when we have just committed to a new career; we hope to be successful in it. But what if you have *faith* that *abundance* is already there? What more do you need? When I looked closely at the image on the 'Faith' card and read its meaning, I knew I was exactly where I needed to be! All I needed was to have *faith* in myself and know that I will always be divinely guided.

The Spirit Creations are some of my favorite Soul Coaching tools. Creating them allowed me to see where my career as a social worker and my passion for being creative all came together. Making a Soul Map Collage allowed me to place in it my intention to manifest the things I wanted in my life. I also made a Spirit Stick from beads, yarn, feathers and natural material and decorated it with love. When I asked the spirit world how to use the stick, I got the answer "With this stick you'll bless the world." This was interesting because on top of my stick I had placed a round ball made out of little branches that I'd found in the garden. It looked just like a world globe. When we had a birthday party during the Soul Coaching program the group decided to make a Spirit Necklace for the birthday girl. She claims that ever since she began wearing that necklace, she has never felt alone anymore. And this has changed her life.

At the end of the 28 day Soul Coaching program it is recommended that you take time out to do a Quest. This involves spending a period of time in a sacred place opening up to the higher self and your inner wisdom, praying and listening for messages. The message that came to me on my Quest was to make a picture book out of the butterfly story. I decided to ask my mother to make illustrations to accompany the story that I had written.

On the day that I had sent her the words to my story, a crop circle in the shape of a huge butterfly appeared within a short distance of my hometown in the Netherlands. Denise Linn talks about how our soul speaks to us through synchronicities, coincidences and signs. For me this sign showed me that I could now trust myself to access the mystical wisdom contained within everyday experiences. And the signs I have received since then have shown me that creating a book will be one of many creative projects. I now trust and have faith that people will benefit from my butterfly story.

The 28 day Soul Coaching program helped me to clear blocks and limitations from my life and allowed me to get in touch with who I really am and what I want to do. It has shown me that there is no reason to compare myself with others and it has made me realize that I have already turned into a beautiful butterfly, ready to spread her wings and fly!

The Colors of Nature

I believe nature is a melding of the elements and none can exist without the other. Being in nature has changed my life. It has given me a place to meditate, the materials to create art, the colors that I choose to wear and the deep healing power and life force that is ever present. Through the air we breathe, the water that cleanses us, the sun that shines its light and warms us and the earth that grounds our feet, the animals that guide us, the plants that nourish us and the trees and stones that provide their wisdom, we create a sense of harmony in our lives.

The 28 day Soul Coaching program is divided into four weeks and each week corresponds with one element. The four elements that we work with are air, water, fire and earth.

During **Air Week** we focus on clearing our mental self. This involves not only clearing clutter around you and in your home, like organizing your kitchen, getting rid of clothes you haven't worn for more than a year, answering e-mails and doing other things you have been putting off. It is also important to clear yourself by speaking your truth, and to assess and evaluate your life and to pay attention to your breathing. When are we breathing and when do we stop breathing and what is the quality of the air we're breathing?

As an Aura-Soma practitioner I integrate a color therapy system that works with the principle: *you are the colors that you choose.* I love to work with the colors of the rainbow that correspond with the seven chakras in our body. An exercise I'd like to share to help you during Air Week is color breathing.

Close your eyes and imagine you're lying in a beautiful place in nature. You see a wonderful rainbow coming out of the earth and arcing up in the sky. Now start to focus on your first chakra at your tailbone. Visualize the color red arcing up from the earth. Breathe out gently and let go of any past anger, frustration or resentment. Breathe in passion, strength awareness and courage. Repeat this three times and notice how it feels. People tend to have a strong reaction to red. Some people may feel highly stimulated, nervous or even angry, while others feel warm and relaxed.

Now move your focus to your second chakra, below your navel. See the color orange arcing up from the earth. Breathe out any past shock or traumas very gently on the out breath. Breathe in the gifts of bliss, insight and creativity. Repeat three times and notice how it feels.

Bring your attention to your third chakra, above your navel. See the color yellow arcing up from the earth. Breathe out and let go of challenges of fear and anxiety. Breathe in light, knowledge and happiness. Imagine it like a beautiful sun with its rays moving through every area of your body. Repeat three times and notice how it feels.

Focus on your fourth chakra, at your chest. Visualize the color green coming directly across the horizon. Breathe out any heaviness that may be lying on the heart. Breathe in the feeling or image of a beautiful scene in nature to find balance and tranquility. Repeat three times and notice how it feels.

Focus on your fifth chakra, at the base of your throat. See the color blue arcing down from the heavens. Breathe out any feelings of responsibilities or burdens you carry on your shoulders. Breathe in peace, patience nurturing and calmness. Visualize the color blue, like the sky without any clouds or a beautiful calm ocean. Repeat three times and notice how it feels

Focus on your sixth chakra, at your third eye, between your eyebrows. See the color indigo arcing down from the heavens. Breathe out any tension and stress that may be in the body and mind. Breathe in intuition and divine love. Repeat three times and notice how it feels.

Now move to the crown on top of your head, your seventh chakra. See the color violet coming directly down from the heavens. Breathe out any tension and stress that may be in the body and mind. Breathe in intuition and divine love. Repeat three times and see how it feels.

During **Water Week** the focus is on clearing your emotional self. For this week I use an exercise where you'll explore your emotional life by coloring your feelings. All you have to do is get out your color pens, pencils and a piece of paper. Put on a CD with nature sounds. An example is the CD series *Spirits of Nature*. Let the music guide you and follow your intuition. You can't do wrong here. If this is hard for you, you can use as a starting point thoughts about your childhood or use your dreams. Try to really communicate from the heart, especially the things that you've always been afraid to say.

During **Fire Week** the focus is on clearing your spiritual self. Your spiritual self will become more apparent to you when you step into trust and faith. You can access this higher power through meditation. In ancient Tibet, as part of a spiritual practice, monks create sand mandalas with colored sand. This action symbolizes the cycle of life. A mandala is an integrated structure organized around a unifying center. Its pattern is also found in nature. You will recognize it for example on the inside of flowers, rings found in tree trunks or in a snail's shell. With the following exercise you can use the fire within to be creative and have fun. Fill seven squeeze bottles with colored sand and use the colors of the rainbow. Create your own mandala pattern. When you're done, take a picture of it to keep as a memory.

During **Earth Week** the focus is on clearing your physical self. A good way to do this is to connect fully with nature and to become more connected to your body. Be aware of the body's physiology by paying attention to how you use your body when you take a walk in nature. The fresh air and a good pace will assist in detoxifying your body. A nice exercise that can be combined while you're walk-ing in nature is to take your camera with you and take pictures of the colors of nature. You can look for the colors that represent the four elements earth, water, air and fire for you. When you come home, you can create a collage using your pictures. These exercises will help you reconnect with your soul and discover what brings it joy!

Healing

AFFIRMATION: Phenomenal healing energy flows through every cell of my body!

Healing is occurring. You're a natural healer. You're on the mend, and/or a situation is being resolved. Have faith that it's happening.

KELLY CHAMCHUK
Coquitlam, BC, Canada

KELLY CHAMCHUK is a compassionate Soul Coach who sees beyond the surface of everyone she encounters. Kelly's warm and inviting presence enables her clients to feel instantly comfortable as she generously offers encouragement. Her ability to connect soul to soul generates productive coaching sessions plus fun and inspirational workshops. Kelly continually develops her intuitive gifts while creating sacred space for others to reach their highest potential.

Receiving her certification from the International Soul Coaching Institute in California in 2008, Kelly constantly expands her abilities with her passion for learning. She gracefully combines her personal life experiences; including training, coaching and facilitation skills from her corporate background with her natural creative flare to guide her clients to live a clutter free, inspired, passionate, heart centered, authentic life of luminosity and love.

Family and friendship comes first. Followed by writing and creating – anything where Kelly can shine some light! There are many stories inside of her, aching to come out including her screenplay; her personal labor of love that will one day make it to the big screen!

Kelly honestly believes that each one of us has the ability to create positive change in the world by altering how we view ourselves first then by influencing others until peace is who we have become. Her message really is about embracing it all with as much passion as you can muster, processing it only with love then letting it all go.

Contact Kelly at www.KellyChamchuk.com

The Wisdom of Spirit Sticks

KELLY CHAMCHUK

Emotions, like baggage . . . carry them with you, only if you must.

*A*rriving in California was like stepping into the life I was supposed to be living, one full of sunshine, fresh air and freedom. "I can breathe here," I thought as I collected my luggage and stood at the car rental booth. The attendant handed me the keys and provided directions to the lot, but I didn't really listen. That happens to me often; little fragments get lost, sometimes important ones. However, I am learning to pay attention. Outside, I walked around and eventually found stall thirteen. A convertible was waiting for me and the sun was shining brightly. What could be better than that?

Though I've learned to pack less over the years, I tend to bring too much. It's the "just in case" syndrome. Ah yes, convertibles and baggage. To enjoy having the roof down, my suitcase would have to go on the back seat. I felt sure it would be 'safe' there. Wondering where that or any of our thoughts come from, I knew I had to get out of my analytical brain and drive! California, here I come!

All I really wanted to do was cruise the California coast. For weeks *that* was the picture in my head. You've heard people say "Be careful what you wish for because you just might get it." Well, I most certainly did! Up and down, North and South along the beautiful sunny California coastline. The scenery was breathtaking with those dramatic cliffs and crashing waves I love so much. I just wanted to *be* there; I had no real idea of where I was going, where to stop, what to see, or what to do. I didn't even have a map. Kind of like my life thus far.

It surprised me how quickly the temperature dropped when the sun went down. I wasn't prepared for that either yet I wanted to keep the top down on the convertible for as long as I could endure it. Even with the heater blasting and my jacket zipped up, I was freezing! Realizing I'd better find my little hotel by the sea before it got too late, I started to focus. There are times when one must stop and ask for directions and this was one of them. I sensed I was heading in the right direction but had allowed doubt to creep in. What if I am wrong? What if I get lost? Oh, I should have planned better; Oh, I should have paid attention; Oh, I am stupid. Maybe I am on the wrong path? "C'mon Kelly, just stop the negative self talk and ask for directions, that's all it means." *Trust.*

After driving past a number of places where I could have stopped and asked but didn't, I finally pulled into a filling station, bought a few snacks to justify 'the ask' then finally asked for directions. Ha, my hotel was right up the road a few miles on the left. They said there is no way you could miss it. I thought, "You don't know *me*." Driving again, I was looking so hard for the building I almost missed the sign for the turnoff. Isn't life just funny that way?

At 8:45 p.m. the sky was mauve. People were lighting fires on the beach. I was surrounded by the beauty of salty air, waves, flames and wait . . . what was that? An earthquake? "Oh God, not now, not while I'm here!" Breathe, just breathe. One of my worst fears ever! Please don't let me create this now. As the grumbling settled, I sat cross-legged on the beach and gave thanks to Mother Earth while looking up at the glorious starscape. I felt I was but one little speck amongst all this grandeur. My inner voice echoed "You are *connected* to this grandeur." I had tears in my eyes absorbing *that* possibility.

There was a mess all around me, blocking my life; I gently stepped out of it, got on the plane and came *here*. But really – I stepped out of my head and back into my heart and soul. I listened to the messages pleading with me to follow my heart. Trusting there was purpose in this desire that had to be explored, I took action and here I was. Not knowing what the future held but *knowing* that this is where the ease is, the grace is, forgiveness, kindness, love, compassion and the truth; everything I could ever imagine I need is already in my heart. *Connect with your heart.*

That connection intensified when arriving at Summerhill Ranch. The welcoming arms of many mothers were on the land and in the winds that chimed through the majestic oak trees. Then there were the motherly arms of Denise Linn, welcoming us all into the healing, nurturing, vibrant energy of her being and her home. Our group was like a brand new family being born simultaneously, brought together again from ancient times to remember passion and love, to learn our lessons and to help ourselves and others heal along the way. I think that is it. *It* – you know – our purpose. To honor our Spirit, our Soul, our Truth, to not be afraid of *who we really are.* But who am I really? It seems some people are born knowing this; they set their minds and they go for it; they live it. They breathe it, do it, and just *are* it. Then there are the ones like me who search and search. It's as if little pieces of the puzzle are in hiding and the purpose of our life is to seek until we find and hopefully not go crazy trying! *Trust the process; timing is divine.*

The lessons went on for days in the sunlit Sanctuary. We broke for nourishing meals and often enjoyed deep relaxation on Soul Journeys to the stars, deep into the oceans, or wherever our Spirit, our Soul needed to go in that moment. We were like apprentices, mastering our craft at an accelerated rate. We learned about turning points in life and the meaning we attach to them.

Ah, turning points. Prior to her suicide, Mom told me she had nothing to live for, not even her children. Hearing that went straight to my heart and crushed it.

Translated, then engrained in my young mind, that meant of course that I was worth nothing and that is how I proceeded to live my life for many years. I choose from that single moment to not be anything like her; not be creative, not be emotional, not get married, not have children, and really – not allow my self to live. So much of *me* left this Earth plane when she left. I lived in pure survival mode or to be completely truthful, self-destructive mode. I forgot I had needs. I forgot I had choice. I certainly forgot about passion and purpose. I forgot about love.

Quite often our early life experiences, the emotions and meanings we attach to them reoccur throughout our lifetime, until we choose to change the meaning and empower ourselves! My issues became loss and abandonment while dancing around with grief, sadness and oh yes, fear. Fear held me hostage. I stuffed these negative emotions inside where they cause disease, like people often do. I was always the *sensitive* one, not only having to deal with my own emotions but often tuning into the emotions of others. Not knowing what this 'sensitivity' was or how to manage the feelings, it was so much easier to just block all emotions out. Or so I thought. Little did I know that as I held on to the loss and the sadness, I was attracting more loss and sadness; therefore the cycle continued. Building the walls to block out others' emotions deprived me of feeling the close connection I so deeply longed for. *Cherish your lessons and embrace all emotions.*

After the end of one particular romantic relationship, followed by the devastating loss of my father, two people with whom I valued a deep connection, I began to have vivid dreams of past lives that explained so clearly what I longed to know. My conscious mind did not always understand, but I would awake with peace, clarity and acceptance from these dreams. Some dreams taught me about the lessons that I agreed to learn in this life, some indicated that I am here to teach or be active in other's lessons and healings. Family members did not always look the same, but *I knew* who they were; I *knew* we were connected then as we are today. Sometimes that was all I really needed to remember. The dreams demonstrated that there is more to life, before we come here and after we leave. *Appreciate your Dreams.*

Wanting to learn more, I decided to study Soul and Past Life Coaching. What I found most empowering was the ability to go back into your past or past lives, then heal, transform and process the experience with love and forgiveness. I'm forever grateful to the lessons and teachers of my life, and to Denise Linn for this gift of bringing peace of mind and most importantly, peace of heart to self and others. It has become part of my blessed journey. Deeply touched by all of the Soul Coaching processes, the process of creating a Spirit Stick became a truly mystical and magical personal experience for me.

Venturing out behind the area called the *Vortex* late in the evening; I was armed with only a flashlight and the stars to guide me. Or so I thought. There was something else there with me; my *self,* so new to me that I am still surprised when she shows up. There were Spirit Guides with me too, very cautious for some reason. They kept me from going deep into the bushes with a sprinkle of fear; similar to how I have lived my life, knowing there was something deep within, yet kept away by fear. The next day I learned there was poison ivy up there! There are times when fear has its place; *listen to the guidance.*

I was on a mission to find a stick that represented *me*. Oh what a challenge. How could I find something when I was just now unearthing the real me? I uncovered a stick clumped together that looked like a three dimensional petrified heart, with all the valves still attached. Though this was quite unsettling, actually freaky, I hung onto it because this might be the one. I kept on looking, just in case.

Walking over to the left side of the Vortex area I discovered an arrow with a yellow feather fletching. This sparked my interest because earlier that day my Past Life Soul Journey had taken me to a time where my life was ended by an arrow in my neck. I had journeyed back in time, gently removed the arrow, healed the wound, and forgiven and blessed all as needed. This was one step in removing fear and doubt, fear of the judgment by others of my words and beliefs, and the judging of oneself – it's all connected. When we visit our past lives we begin to see recurring patterns. One of mine was about speaking – speaking my truth, without fear of crucifixion! *Speak your truth gently.*

Picking up the broken arrow and holding this gift from the universe I thought "Maybe this is my stick," yet I continued my search. Finding another stick, it felt like a 'good' size so I added it to my growing collection. Then for whatever reason, I was guided to look on the right side of the Vortex and found a stick there that represented exactly what I was *feeling*. Symbolically heart shaped, but not as grotesque looking as the stumpy one, this one had a few branches off a strong main branch and one extra spindly twig. I tried to yank this little branch off but it would not break. That's when I knew. *This is me.* I set all my twigs on the porch of the Vortex Room to let them rest in the moonlight that night. Sometimes final decisions can wait until they're ready to be made.

In the morning, with newfound intention, I took the gross heart-like stump and tossed it deep into the cluster of Vortex trees, freeing myself from my petrified heart, throwing it back to the universe to become reborn, perhaps into something more viable. Collecting my perfect branch and arrow, I decided to combine them into one Spirit Stick.

Beautiful beads and exquisite yarns were laid out on the dining table for the group to work with. I gathered into a bowl what I thought I might use to decorate my stick. Just like my life again, I found myself thinking that I must have everything in the bowl first before beginning. I intentionally chose my beads, selecting each with purpose and symbolic meaning: the colors, shapes, textures, and one with etchings to represent the emotional scars I am healing. It wasn't so much about re-opening old wounds, it was more about healing and releasing the emotions, unlocking their cages and setting them free! I carried everything outside near the fountain. Water Week in the Soul Coaching Program is all about emotional cleansing. It felt important to be out in nature, near the flowing, primal, cleansing, rejuvenating properties of the sacred healing element – water.

Creating a Spirit Stick is a ceremony that brings clarity to events in our life, or changes our perception about those events. I performed a silent blessing ritual, welcoming the purifying Spirit of Water, thanking my emotions for serving their purpose and bringing their lessons and truths, however painful. I set my intention to heal my past of all pain and suffering as I continued to work with the 'heart theme' that was evolving. "I am going to heal my heart. Today is the day. Spirit, show me how."

The stick did represent my heart; I noticed it more and more as I played away. The strong branch represented my Aorta valve, damaged from severe Rheumatic Fever as a child. My heart really has been through a lot in this lifetime, physically and emotionally, I consciously acknowledged. The arrow, along with the symbolism from the previous Soul Journey spoke to me. The message: *Allow love to pierce my heart.* I recorded each thought, action and feeling in my journal, like a scientist about to make an important discovery. I began to tie the arrow to the center of the stick and thought "heartstrings!" One string represented the past, the other the future. Every step from then on originated from the center and spread outwards. Heartstrings like a spider's web, connected, Heart Centered. This felt so appropriate.

Drawn to work with the 'past' string first, I began to decorate and heal it with each bead that I deliberately threaded on. The black bead at the bottom was to remind me that although I've spent time in the darkness I am moving towards the light. I continued with green healing beads, tiny pink stars and some crystal, each one representing a life experience that desired a touch of healing. With each

> **Embracing**
>
> *AFFIRMATION: I embrace and love all of my life*
>
> *Embrace all of your life, both the dark and the light. Dance with your shadow, and reclaim parts of yourself that you've denied. Embrace your past and what has been hidden or denied.*

bead I momentarily connected with the emotion of the event; determining where I held it in my body, honoring how it steered my life, and yes, appreciating the aliveness whole-heartedly. All those emotions, those lessons, those *teachers* . . . So much has been learned in this lifetime. I was not erasing the memory and everything attached, I was embracing the memory and letting go. Water week is the time to wash it all away, to cleanse and rejuvenate. I allowed my tears to flow. A message 'arrived,' *each one of us is an exquisite pearl,* so I placed a pearl close to the center. It takes a long time to create a pearl so beautiful.

The 'future' string welcomed seashells, reminding me to be open, allow the tides in and out, and to just *be* the vessel. It glistened with shiny beads reflecting the light and contained open space to permit room for new and exciting things to enter my life. There were bright green leaves to signify growth and at the end, a large peachy colored, opalescent bead representing where we go when we are finished with this life, back to the warm, cozy, loving womb of the universe. *Embrace the cycle of life.*

I wound the furry green yarn around the center of the stick, each time around intentionally bringing healing to my core, my soul. Green, beautiful green, how I love the color of the heart chakra, the color of springtime, the color of growth! Drawn also to a soft natural colored yarn, it reminded me there is strength in softness. I chose brilliantly colored yarn with multicolored fabric bobbles to be wrapped around that Aorta branch. This branch somehow symbolized my future. It had color everywhere! How fun! "Maybe this yarn chose me," I thought and smiled.

The sun was getting terribly hot but I didn't care. Extremely thirsty, and remembering it is important to stay hydrated, especially during Water Week, I ventured inside to fetch a glass of cold water and decided to put back some of the beads; they were not what I truly wanted after all. It's interesting that there can be clutter clearing even when creating a Spirit Stick! Learning not to question, I was going with the flow. Glancing towards the dining table I actually noticed different colors of yarn there. Were they there from the beginning and I had not noticed? Oh, how often has *that* happened in my life?

On the garden path I gathered some beautiful fresh fragrant lavender that was waving to me in the breeze and picked up an acorn lying on the ground, both screaming to be a part of this process. Approaching the fountain I observed some interesting plants growing from the rock wall. Why was I witnessing all this now? I gently pulled some of the growth out and thanked it also for being part of my Spirit Stick. *Beautiful things can grow from hard places.* "Things like me?" I wondered aloud, looking around to see who I was talking to. *Grow and flourish!*

We were nearing the end of our allotted time and I still had so much more I wanted to accomplish. I hoped this would not be my story in 'real life' so quickened my pace. *Cherish your time.* Continuing on with the nature theme, I picked up the acorn, examined it then tied it near the core, the center of my heart. This blossoming shape is there to encourage me to emerge. I could feel my real heart growing and expanding. You don't have to wait for healing to happen, *it is happening*! Growing more excited, I decided to tie an additional string dropping down from the now strong Aorta branch. This 'extension of my heart' had three circular shells, each to honor past, present and future, as well as mind, body and spirit!

While I was admiring, not criticizing, the evolution of my Spirit Stick, a beautiful butterfly fluttered right in front of me. She etched her message in the sky – a giant figure eight pattern, leaving me with the beautiful message *infinity*. Everything in the universe seems to contain a message if you choose to see or hear it. I thanked the winged creature from my newly healed heart as she flew away, off towards the majestic Grandfather Tree. "It *could* happen," I argued with my logical mind.

I came to that tiny little twig that couldn't be broken. It looked fragile, like it would just snap, yet it didn't. It felt vulnerable yet strong at the same time. Intuitively I took a strand of a baby pink yarn and began gently winding it around and around, not wanting to smother. The result was a beautiful tiny cocoon. A safe place, somewhere to go until the transformation is complete. Just then I paused and understood why the butterfly had come. I held up the aromatic lavender, inhaled deeply a few times then tied the sprigs on tight. Whoever wrote "take time to stop and smell the roses" did not have Summerhill lavender nearby!

My Spirit Stick was not completed that day. There were many loose ends and they were driving me crazy – loose ends, just like life. During a meditation I went *into* my Spirit Stick and asked about the loose ends. The message was: *learn to live and find peace with the loose ends; they will be tied up in divine time.* There is so much wisdom in the Spirit Stick. It wasn't until many weeks later at home that I finally returned to complete it. I placed a beautiful crystal onto the heart center area for clarity. To the Aorta branch I glued a gemstone dragonfly, a beautiful gift from a fellow Soul Coach. *It is time for my Spirit to soar, from the waters to the wind.*

Like that old petrified heart I threw back to the universe, part of me stayed at Summerhill, not like trash left behind, but more like a recycling of the soul. It was a clutter clearing of the spirit. I had created sacred space in my heart and soul for newness to arrive; seeds were planted, so wisdom, compassion and love would grow.

With each stick I now see created and each story I hear, my heart expands. I love to witness the freedom that occurs when others share their personal stories and am deeply touched as truth surfaces in sacred space. It's such a simple yet profound process to combine nature, art and healing. Human emotions may separate us from any other creature on this planet, however they are what connects us as *humans be-ing.*

Creating Your Own Spirit Stick

The best time to create a Spirit Stick is when you have something you wish to heal or something you want to create. Soul Journey in meditation and set your intention for what you want to achieve and go for it! Make sure your stick is dry and take time to find the one that truly represents you in this moment. Driftwood, sticks, twigs; anything goes! If you are wondering if size matters, well – in this case, no. The size of the stick in no way corresponds to the size of the Spirit! What matters is the meaning you attach to the process. This is a positive turning point, a time to heal or create. Let go of your emotional baggage, releasing that which no longer serves you. Change the meaning to something that serves you in a positive way – create a glorious memory.

Consciously choose objects you wish to be a part of the process. Utilize materials from nature like rocks, moss, shells and feathers as well as beautiful beads, yarns, fabrics and personal items that have meaning for you. Note the colors and textures you are drawn to. Apply objects that you *connect* with, that you *love*. Glue them on; tie them on; wrap them on, whatever works – just do it! Open all of your senses. Allow your creativity to flow like the water! Surrender to the process. Begin where you *feel, sense, know;* just go with the flow! Journal as you proceed; record your thoughts, feelings and *messages* without judgment. It adds priceless value to this discovery process.

Everything that happens is happening for a reason – explore it with curiosity! Take time to ask your stick what *it* wants and honor those requests as they hold much wisdom for you. Be the sacred observer of everything that occurs *around* you, but more so of what is going on *inside* of you. Try doing this project silently so you can focus on your feelings. This is what Water Week is all about! Laugh. Stomp. Cry. Encourage your emotions to bubble to the surface with grace, *now*, in this sacred moment. Ask yourself, "If not now, when?" Affirm that this day is the day to heal, create and move on. "It's happening!"

Your Spirit Stick may be complete in one sitting or it may be a work in progress that evolves in divine time. Once done, set it out to cleanse overnight in the moonlight, under the shimmering stars. Mine hangs proudly on my wall as a reminder. You will *know* what to do to honor yours. Close with a Soul Journey to become 'one' with your Spirit Stick; hold it in your hands, infuse its soul with love; then sit back and allow it to do the same for yours.

Illuminate your soul with love.

Miracles

AFFIRMATION: My life is a miracle!

*Miracles occur in your life
every day. Watch for and
embrace them. As you notice
and accept the small wonders in
your life, greater gifts will grow
in abundance all around you.*

MISASHA
Ontario, Canada

MISASHA – THE SAGE SPIRIT, a.k.a. J. Gean Hemming, continues to live life experientially. An adventurer and world traveler, she has been from Greenland to Australia – plus numerous places in between – Machu Picchu, Mexico, Ireland. . . . She holds a degree in English and Psychology and has flown in two Angel Derbys (All Women's International Air Races). She is filled with gratitude for support from Mighty Forces as well as the daily whisperings from her Soul. She is trying her vigilant best to not let any static interfere with reception!

Volunteering at a day-long workshop by Denise Linn in April 2006 led her to Denise's next Soul Coaches training – SC17. There was one spot left, but that was all she needed! Her life and the lives of many around her have been strengthened as a result.

A near-death experience at age 20, life's opportunities-for-growth, chosen learnings, and a love of books have all helped mould her perception of life . . .and the here-after. Resolution and details of her current dark-night-of-the-soul will be forthcoming. She's not quite sure when or in what format, but she has a heaping-helping of Faith to sustain her!!

Her affirmation: Let Right Prevail. Thy Will be done. "Let Right Prevail" is the motto of the Law Society of Upper Canada.

Contact: TheSageSpirit@gmail.com

Life's Crucible – Alchemy's Moment of Truth

MISASHA

*As human beings our greatness lies
not so much in being able to remake the world,
as in being able to remake ourselves.*

— GANDHI

'*H*is perceptive abilities can bring to light all those special qualities that lie within you,' the flyer proclaimed. It said he had 'over 25 years experience.' Hmm, I wondered. It was November 29, 2009 and I was about to test the perceptive skills of a psychically intuitive male 'life-coach,' from India.

Still in the estate-saga's grip, which had recently spawned a Claim for Damages, I was ready to try *almost* anything! Was it remotely possible that his 'perceptive abilities' might provide some useful information?

His sharings and observations did prove to be insightful. I gleaned several reminders and admonitions: "You're to listen to your intuition . . . most of all, stop over-analyzing. You are trying to magnify your problems too much in your head . . . there's a lot of stress which is not good for you."

"Hmm" snorted my super-reasonable *judge-interpreter*. "Did you really need a psychic to tell you that stress was not good for you? Didn't that *shingles* episode two months ago give you that message?" I had to acknowledge that this was so.

"You're very intelligent and practical" he went on "*but*, you're not listening to the emotional side of you. Unfortunately you just listen to your logic; you don't listen to your intuition."

"Emotional side!" cringed my *judge-interpreter*. "What's wrong with being 'logical' and 'super-reasonable' . . . like me?" I began listening more intently to the insightful sharings for which I was paying.

"So, only working hard and being an efficient robot is not good. You have to *vent* . . . you don't *vent*! Therefore, you are to transform yourself."

I was in wholehearted agreement. Transformation *was* needed. I was ready for change! Three years of lack of closure and of being an efficient robot was taking a heavy toll, I reflected, acknowledging that I had become too fixedly-focused. So often we can't see in ourselves, what we can so clearly see in others. His perceptions were appreciated.

And the day came when the risk to remain in a tight bud
was more painful than the risk it took to bloom.

—ANAIS NIN

The largest and heaviest rose bud I had ever seen or held, was given to me during my time in Ecuador. Located within 12 km of the Equator, Quito is the world supplier of long stem roses – each being harvested at the peak of its unswerving upward trajectory seeking its light source. My gifted bud was heavy with promise. Carefully and with appreciation I took it to my apartment, placing it in a vase of water. Expectation and anticipation were difficult to rein in, knowing that the rose's crimson velvet sheath would pale once its heart had reached full expression.

That bud provided a huge reminder: things are not always as we perceive them to be or as we anticipate. The rose bud seemed hesitant. Indecision and restraint were evident as it held its velvet red petals tightly wrapped about itself – as a cold and weary wayfarer might on a long and bitter windy trek. It gave occasion for reflection. The bud, imbued and with immense proportion and potential, never did open. Slowly and in silence it slid into decay, taking its unexpressed gift with it.

Candice Pert, Professor of Physiology and Biophysics says in *Molecules of Emotion,* that our body/mind and our very cells are held together by the "glue" of our emotions. And since "emotions run every system of your body, [don't] underestimate their power to contribute to health or disease."

You know your glue is losing its grip when, at 01:45 in the wee hours of the morning, you tell your word perfect *paperclip* (office-assistant) to "*Bleep* off!" as with unnerving insistence his little paper-clip tail is incessantly clanging in discordant cacophony, to get your attention to offer unwanted assistance. Maybe that's how *losing one's grip* was coined . . . or maybe not. Anyway, I admit that my knee-jerk verbal expletive was out of character for Ms. Perfection. However, relief came in that moment when I didn't suppress my mounting frustration . . . and just *vented*! A start I figured, towards "not being an efficient robot." Why, it even felt *good*! I smiled though my sleep-deprived senses.

Alchemy is chemistry's medieval predecessor. It tried to achieve some audaciously heady accomplishments. On the material level it tried to transmute base metals into gold. On a spiritual level, the task was to achieve enlightenment and eternal life. Associated with philosophy and magic, it engaged in a seemingly miraculous power or course of action to change one thing into something better. Transmutation!

Is it any wonder then that the ever changing, transmutable and alchemical properties of Water have been traditionally associated with our equally ever-changing, transmutable and alchemical emotional self? Water, like our emotional self, reacts to the 'heat' of the moment and becomes a vaporous cloud of imperceptible droplets of moisture. Reacting to cold it mirrors, with chilling similarity, the frosty demeanor of our sometimes emotional self. In its most natural state it 'goes-with-the' and flows effortlessly and with ease – so like another facet of our emotional self. Ninety percent of a fetus and upwards of seventy percent of an adult's physical makeup is water.

In the early 1990s, Japanese water researcher, Masuro Emoto demonstrated graphically that water responds to human thoughts and prayers. It even responds to the written and spoken word! He used distilled water as the control – having no 'imprint.' Homeopathic remedies, conversely, retain the *vibrational imprint* of the original substance from which they are created, although no perceptible or measurable part of the original substance remains. These are inspirational mysteries of the world that we call "home."

Home – a reminder that I've been *homeless* since being forced to sell my three bedroom townhouse in June 2007! I became a wandering 'researcher,' seeking truth and justice. It led me into life's alchemical crucible – a transformative process using the soul's *dark-night*.

Society irrevocably impacts each 'clean-slate' as it comes into the world. Descriptions of me as a child: cute, capable, caring and compliant. I was seasoned-by-reason at an early age: a gentle soul, choosing to be born between two lightening-rods (an older, by 2 ¾ years brother and a younger, by 3 years sister). Athletically gifted and loving to learn new things, this gentle soul loved activity and knowledge. Sponge-like, she devoured her older brother's school lessons; eagerly taught by her Mom. By grade five, she and her brother were in the same class.

An endearing source of pride for her parents, she was unintentionally and unknowingly being nurtured as a *human-doing* and a perfectionist. The parents' golden haired dream-child would soon forget her true nature as she reveled and basked in the attention and adulation being heaped upon her. Name it and she would try to do it and, in most instances she succeeded. Soon the *performer* saw her reflection in adoring eyes – lovingly being placed on a pedestal. Thus began the gentle soul's quest to reconnect with her *true* nature, for she also brought with her self-reliance and psychological might.

Nature and nurture . . . clean-slates are soon written upon by the world that surrounds. When we fail to wipe clear the perceptions and beliefs that are not resonant with our soul's truth it makes for a disquieted Spirit. On this I may be quoted: perfection is a pointless pursuit! And yet, many like me, conditioned from an early age, pursue it. It has taken me six decades to more fully realize the folly. With a seeking mind, openness and power of insight we give 'something better,' or *transmutation*, an opportunity to birth – spiritual alchemy via the Element of Water!

Early January 2010, I gave eight lawyers (yes, eight), a deadline. "Before January 18, 2010," my email told them quite unequivocally, "I need resolution *and* . . . it must have integrity!" (It is now January 17, 2010.)

My latest *Soul Collages*, filled with heart-felt desires and wishes shouted out to the Creator of All-that-is. I pleaded with the angelic realm, through words cut from magazines – "Enough with waiting" . . . "its time" . . . "Out with the old" . . . "change-angels" . . . "walking tall, angel magic" . . . "can do" "ask . . . let . . . gratitude" . . . "With God all things are possible." . . ."balance" . . . "resilient . . . peace of mind."

"Help!" I was surrendering. I had learned the lesson of my own human frailty. Perhaps you can identify with my foolhardiness i.e. *'my* will be done.' I know that I have need for intercession, consultation and help from the most powerful celestial recruits known to and created for humanity. Archangel Michael, for example, is patron Saint of the Toronto Police Force and is revered! I poured forth into my collages as much humility as I could, noting some of my human transgressions and being sure to *ask* for Divine and angelic intervention. 'Asking,' you must realize, is more than merely a pious-platitude!

Perhaps you recall my 'life-altering 2001 experience' in the first *Soul Whispers* book when Mighty Forces, rousing to my rescue, came to my aid – miraculously providing u.s. $24,001 – one dollar more than needed! How easy though, in our *super-reasonable ego-minded* humanness, to forget such miracles that keep hope and optimism alive for us. When life for us becomes mechanical, mundane and routinely-rote, our intuitive-knowingness is squelched. It cannot thrive. It becomes lost. Humanity, however, is gifted with resilience. We *can* regroup, learning methods and/or tools to empower ourselves. Soul Coach training gave me some powerful tools. For example: Soul Collages – something akin to a visual prayer; and Time Lines – a reflective tool whereby you review life's turning points and defining moments. Although we may experience transformation, have we been transmuted into "something better"? Each of us, alone, holds that answer.

If you read my Chapter in *Soul Whispers*, you would know that 'external circumstances' in November 2006, provided me with the opportunity to stand my ground in spite of overwhelming personal and financial challenges, and to speak out about injustice and lack of integrity by those in positions of trust, influence, and perceived external power. This rather 'politically correct' statement is quite impotent in describing the impact and *grit* of the emotional mayhem that resulted.

Beneath my simmering, seething self-righteous indignation were the emotions of anger, frustration and sadness: anger at the estate's shielding of truth through

---

Breakthrough

AFFIRMATION: I soar with limitless love, light, and joy!

You're at the precipice of a huge, positive breakthrough! Everything that you've been doing for the past few years has been preparing you for this time. An immense self-realization is on its way. Something for which you've waited a long time is about to come to fruition!

an adamant, heels-dug-in reluctance to mediate, talk or listen to reason (as I saw it). I was frustrated and angry that my film project was being jeopardized and at the 11th hour had to be aborted. Anger is like the outer layer of an onion. Through peeling away each layer, the *heart* of the matter begins to reveal itself. Seldom will you find any anger. For me, I found sadness. I was sad knowing that my 'ex' had crossed over not knowing the truth. I was sad that my children had not only recently lost their dad, but were now losing their mom (due to misinformation).

In less than 12 hours it will be my birthday. I've always loved having another birthday. It certainly beats the alternative!

Everything on earth has its own time.
There is an opportune time to do all things –
a right time for everything.

—SONG OF SOLOMON

My daughter's email birthday card, January 18, 2007, was true to her nature – creative, clever, and cute. There's a big *but*, though; tomorrow will be three years since I received a birthday card from my daughter – born three weeks before my birthday, some 30 years ago. I am saddened at having needlessly lost those three years, even though my rational self tells me that life's extreme challenges offer opportunities to grow and strengthen. It is life, however, that chooses when and what opportunities will set us on a path of potential growth and strengthening. Seemingly this is one of the rules in the game-of-life. In reviewing the Hebrew bible experiences of Job I've been working at honing his virtues – still working! I reminded the mighty Creator that I didn't really think I needed to go any further into Job's experiences. I mean, isn't my recent immune-suppressed episode with shingles and a near-death experience at age 20 enough? Not to mention the three year estate-saga!

The Q'ero Indians, guardians of ancient wisdom and descendants of the last refugee of Incan nobility, know that the initiate's route to becoming a *paqo* (shaman) is only possible through one's personal experiences. How can our Spirit sing or our Soul soar when tethered to the beliefs and perceptions of others, accepted as our own? Wisdom comes from living *our* experiences. Unlike knowledge, wisdom cannot be taught.

My Soul Collages were burgeoning with heart, soul and emotion. "Everything is on the table" . . . "the time is now . . ." "make sense" . . . "feud-free plan" . . . "mend fences" . . . "Ready, set, Birthday wish" (I was upping the ante) . . . "Win-Win" . . . "Blessed Unity." Well, yesterday was the January 18th deadline. No response from the lawyers. Drat!

Like our emotions, water may display and take on many countenances: an effortless and easy-flowing stream meandering through a meadow; an ethereal morning mist – like a down-filled duvet being lifted from a secluded mountain lake by the sun; a wedding gowned frothiness flow of white water rapids; the fearlessness of a downhill skier's racer-like descent of a mountain stream gurgling, chortling, and carving with cavalier and effortless ease around moguls; or, the cool yet hard and unyielding reserve of winter's frozen constrictiveness. Each of our emotions, from the heights of joy, passion and exuberance, to the depths of sorrow, despair and grief are necessary to give life *contrast*, and the *balance* needed for *wholeness*.

All sun makes for a desert.

—ARAB PROVERB

As an aerobatic pilot I have joy-filled recollections of the exuberant and care-free, but disciplined-abandon experienced during aerobatic maneuvers. Thus, with delight and passion, I strongly identify with the poem of the 19-yr-old WWII Spit-fire pilot, written three months before his death:

Oh! I have slipped the surly bonds of Earth
And danced the skies on laughter-silvered wings;
Sunward I've climbed, and joined the tumbling mirth
Of sun-split clouds, – and done a hundred things
You have not dreamed of – wheeled and soared and swung
High in the sunlit silence. Hov'ring there,
I've chased the shouting wind along, and flung
My eager craft through footless hall of air. . . .
Up, up the long delirious burning blue
I've topped the wind-swept heights with easy grace
Where never lark, or ever eagle flew –
And, while with silent, lifting mind I've trod
The high untrespassed sanctity of space.
Put out my hand, and touched the face of God.

–High Flight BY JOHN GILLESPIE MCGEE JR.

Overwhelming and ecstatic emotional resonance floods my being as I *experience* this poem. It is a soul resonance and a recollection of the Divine spark that burns within each being – and which shines forth when the *judge-interpreter* is not at the controls. Sadness, anger, despair, grief, etc. represent some of the programs selected and run by the emotions. Likened to muddy spring-time ruts, they reside in the back-fields of our minds – becoming ever more ingrained, imbedded, and deepened with use. As with a digital camera, if you selectively accept/select some emotions yet deny/suppress or delete others you are left lacking and unbalanced.

Consider the following: 'In memoriam' to an 80-yr-old psychiatrist: Divorced at age 52, he was the medical superintendent of a psychiatric hospital. And yet, at age 69, following the death of his second partner, he "sank into a depression" from which "the physician could not heal himself." Another told of a "brilliant and promising young doctor," 23-years-old, who apparently died by suicide, "from the pain of loss." This "profound lesson" taught his brothers that "being young, he could only see the present and not beyond; not yet understanding that life moves in cycles, in waves that ebb and flow, often gently, but sometimes with tremendous force, like the powerful tides of the ocean." Both tragically reveal that neither education nor innate intelligence nor age has a positive correlation to emotional intelligence.

> *It is right it should be so:*
> *Man was made for joy and woe;*
> *And when this we rightly know*
> *Through the world we safely go.*
> *Joy and woe are woven fine,*
> *A clothing for the soul divine.*
>
> *—Auguries of Innocence* BY WILLIAM BLAKE

Remember always: although you have emotions, you are *not* your emotions. Emotions in all their intensity come and go. You, however, remain. Water, traditionally, represents mankind's emotional facet – also symbolizing intuition, trust, nurturing, dreams, and innocence.

"Do you want to come home?" It was my mom. I was 28-yrs old, living and working 550 miles from 'home.' I had my pilot's license and was furthering my flying qualifications on weekends and after hours from my Federal Government nine to five. I had the proverbial world-by-the-tail! And now, in a matter of but a single heart-beat, death had extinguished the life-force of my fiancé – three days after Christmas! The joy and happiness that surrounds Christmas became, in that one heart-beat, inconsolable grief. As my world imploded, tears of disavowing-disbelief, and seemingly bottomless sorrow engulfed me. Unknowingly, at the time, I erected a protective wall around my heart.

> *I had a daily bliss*
> *I half indifferent viewed*
> *Till suddenly I perceived it stir-*
> *It grew as I pursued,*
> *Till when, around a crag*
> *It wasted from my sight*
> *Enlarged beyond my utmost scope,*
> *I learned its sweetness right.*
>
> *—Lost Joy* BY EMILY DICKINSON

Time, it's said is a healer of all wounds and slowly my life once more took on color. I later married and our daughter was born *three* days after Christmas – the 7th anniversary of my fiancé's death. God's gentle mercy!

It's been quite a journey these past three years – from being '115 lbs of seething self-righteous-indignation' to a more accepting being, through understanding – yes, of others, but more importantly of myself. I'm still a work-in-progress – becoming more integrated, whole, and balanced – accepting, feeling and running the gauntlet of humanity's emotional repertoire, which Denise reminds ". . . allow us to experience life in all its fullness and richness." I want to live life filled with a plethora of rich, succulent and varied experiences – testing and strengthening my mettle. Hindsight, however, reveals that life gave me exactly those experiences these past three years. Life's crucible-firing has strengthened and transmuted knowledge into wisdom – the like of which I could neither have bought nor otherwise have learned.

> *Meditate. Live Purely. Be quiet.*
> *Do your work with mastery.*
> *Like the moon, come out from behind the clouds. Shine!*
>
> —BUDDHA

My super-reasonable, know-it-all, holier-than-thou, *judge-interpreter* never knew, as it passionately ranted on, that Forces behind life's façade were working intently but patiently – not to rush me, but to take me 'home for the holidays.'

My vision, however, had been along the lines of finally leaving the nomadic lifestyle behind. Circumstances obliged me, as noted in my *Soul Whispers* Chapter: "Saying YES to Life . . . in spite of Seeming Impossibilities" to sell my 3 bedroom townhouse in June 2007, and consequently left me in the world of having no-fixed-address; and becoming a homeless gypsy-researcher seeking truth and justice.

I was now becoming fixated on once more having my *own* place. You know – a physically created solid structure, a permanent dwelling – something with a roof and four walls, with a fully-equipped kitchen, living room, office/den, bedrooms, bathrooms, even room for guests – something with a street name, a mailbox . . .. a storage area even!

The 'home' that was being prepared for me, during my nomadic quest for truth and justice in the great world around me, could neither be bought nor sold. It was of exquisite yet priceless beauty – a home filled with peace and unfathomable serenity and joy. No amount of money or wealth could purchase it. Any yet, it was being gifted to me!

My soul's dark night was coming to an end. Life had become the alchemist's crucible in which the alchemical transmutation could take place. My base metal underwent the alchemical change through the Universal-solvent: Water's emotional release, through feelings. The shedding of tears of both joy and sorrow revealed a heart of greater love, understanding, and compassion.

Humanity, insisting on having free-will, was thus gifted with such by the Creator/Great Mystery/Allah/Jehovah. Unfortunately, the *judge-interpreter* has been hogging the reins; and becoming its own little free-will, power-driven, small 'g' god. During my journey towards a measurable plot of land, I seemingly have come full circle: infinity . . . life . . . death . . . rebirth (transmuted into 'something better' within life's alchemical crucible).

> *Our birth is but a sleep and a forgetting:*
> *The Soul that rises with us, our life's Star,*
> *Hath had elsewhere its setting,*
> *And cometh from afar:*
> *Not in entire forgetfulness,*
> *And not in entire nakedness,*
> *But trailing clouds of glory do we come*
> *From God, who is our home.*

—WILLIAM WORDSWORTH

May you be equally blessed.

To Thine Own Self Be True

Know thyself read the sign, over the portal through which one passed, en route to consult the Oracle at Delphi. Shakespeare also counseled that only when one is true to oneself, can one be true to another.

Yet we see, with supercilious clarity of knowingness, in *others* what we fail to see with the same clarity of assuredness within our own selves. It is not possible to be true to our *Self* if we do not know who *we* are. Shakespeare has a point, *n'est-ce pas?*

More often than not, though, our lives may have taken on such a frenetic and busy bent that seldom do we have the time *or* energy to consider *any* sign imploring us to become inwardly reflective.

Seldom, if ever, do we gift ourselves with true introspective meditation. A period of soul-searching contemplation was gifted to me some four plus years ago – though neither consciously nor deliberately by choice.

My reliance upon making Soul Coaching Collages – journeying within and allowing my Soul's expression to materialize – has helped me to gain insightful-understanding, courage, and serenity.

Let's now set aside a block of time, by choice this moment, to learn about Soul Coaching Collages.

A simple explanation of the process: it's the gathering of photos, phrases, words, images (from various sources) and, *with intention,* gluing them on a piece of poster or heavier board (preferably white says Denise). There is a synergy of magical proportions that occurs when you are part of a group; as in a Soul Coaching Workshop with a certified Soul Coach. Although the group is working individually it also is working collectively – for it is a *process*, not a *technique*.

Here's How:

1. As you allow your intuition free reign, and without forethought, dive right in and begin to clip, gather, and accumulate what, for you, has a *resonant-ring*. Only you will know.

2. Once gathered, place, without gluing, the images, words, phrases where they *seem* to fit or belong on the poster board.

3. Shift, shuffle, change and move the items around, until everything looks and *feels* just-right. Again, you will know.

4. Glue time: with deliberation glue everything in its consciously-chosen and deliberately-perfect place – there are no errors!

5. Now: 'ta-da', for the review. Prop or set it directly in front of you so that you can look intently into what you and your inner-knowingness have just created. At this point the Certified Soul Coach would take you on a Soul Journey *into* the Collage to uncover even greater insights of understanding and awareness.

6. Hang it in a prominent location where you see it often. Soon the deeper energy of the images, words and phrases will begin to resonate within your consciousness.

Denise notes: "there are as many different types of collages as there are intentions." In addition to self-exploration, some are for divination, while others are for creation and manifestation.

Remember that *you* alone can truly interpret your collage. The Soul Coach, however, will be able to share the interpretive method Denise created (having taught collages to thousands of people for 37 years) whereby the collage is loosely divided into nine sections – providing "mystical messages for you from your subconscious and your Soul."

For example: my latest collage has the full vertebrae running up the entire left side. The meanings that follow are the questions that have *resonated* with me: "What seeds do I want to germinate for the future?"; "What is being nurtured within me at this time?" and "What is the most powerful intention I can hold for myself at this time?" A perfect fit, for I'll no doubt need lots of *backbone* for next Friday's court appearance, with *potentially* five opposing lawyers.

Top center are the words "solution Archangel Michael" . . . "perfect angel chemistry" . . . "together we can" . . . "erase controversy" "top my account." My meaning:" What do my Guides/Angels/Spirit Allies want me to know at this time?" Another perfect fit: I feel a close connection with the angelic realm and particularly to Archangel Michael.

Enjoy the *process*.

Opening

Affirmation: I am open to receiving the gifts of the universe!

Be open to receive the gifts of the universe. There's nothing to fear, so allow your vulnerability to shine. Fling your arms to the heavens and exclaim, "I'm ready!" Stretch, expand, and venture forth: Doors of opportunity are opening for you!

DEB SWINGHOLM
Chiang Mai, Thailand

BORN IN OHIO, USA, Deb Swingholm has lived in Asia and the Middle East since 1997. She is currently settled in Chiang Mai, Northern Thailand, with her husband Greg and a sparrow called Grace.

From this beautiful setting, Deb's lifelong passion for art, music and spiritual discovery continues to take her around the world. Her journey encompasses sacred sites and mystical places as she gathers knowledge of ancient traditions, shamanic practices, ceremonies and healing methods drawn from many cultures.

Her study of Sacred Space and the relationship between art, nature and spirituality – the interconnectedness of all things – continues today. A Master Teacher of Feng Shui and Space Clearing, Deb is also a Soul Coach, Reiki teacher and gifted intuitive, with nearly 20 years experience of working in the field of personal development and transformation. Ethereal, like her artwork, Deb has a unique and graceful way of guiding others in listening to their own inner wisdom and "connecting with the Goddess within."

Through stunning photography, Deb reveals an appreciation for the divine that is imminent in each moment and, as in all her work, communicates a deep spiritual insight.

By honoring the Divine Feminine and women's spirituality and sacred traditions, Deb helps to cultivate a sacred space in one's heart and home. She is currently working on a seminar series called "Walking with the Goddess."

To contact Deb, visit www.FloweringMoon.com

Sacred River, Holy Well

DEB SWINGHOLM

Healing, purification, abundance and blessings,
This is what I offer you.
I am Water.
I give birth to all life.
I am the ocean within you.

—A MESSAGE FROM WATER

With the sun setting over a distant, rocky ochre-colored outcrop, I settle back into the cushions as our boat slides along, silently pushed by the wind on this magnificent river. The mysteries of this place unfold around me as the great Nile moves beneath me.

Sailing along this ancient watercourse, I am amazed by the intensity of color on the riverbanks. On either side is a thin strip of vibrant, rich green. Beyond that, sand; dry, arid dunes and rock. The life-giving nature of water is more visible here than perhaps anywhere else I have been. Bountiful life flourishes in this crease of moisture. All along the fertile banks of the river, irrigation canals feed small farmer's plots. Sugar cane and palm trees grow tall. Animal corrals lean against tiny mudbrick houses. Men and young children fish with nets cast from small boats.

The Nile, like so many other rivers, symbolizes *life* itself. Pouring forth nourishment, she sustains all things.

As the scene changes with the movement of our boat, temples come into view. Many of Egypt's temples were built at the banks of this sacred river. Disembarking our felucca, I ascend the steps leading up from the river to the outer gates of one of these temples. As I walk the ancient stone pathways, moving between the tall carved columns, approaching the inner chambers of the Holy of Holies, I feel even more deeply the sanctity and sacredness of this river. I easily imagine the elaborate processions from the water's edge into the temple courtyard, accompanied by the smells of flowers, herbs, frankincense and myrrh, and the sound of sistrums. I visualize the rich offerings of grain, beer, honey, dates and bread – all conceived by the gift of water, and offered back in thanks.

Sacred Water

Since ancient times, we humans have had great reverence for water. There is a sacredness with which we hold her. In nearly every culture there is ceremony, religious ritual and seasonal celebrations that reflect our enormous respect for water and our strong belief in its potent healing qualities. Water symbolizes a union of the spiritual and the physical realms. It represents cleansing; purification of body and spirit. And, it is seen as the source of abundance and blessings.

Water is also symbolic of birth and creativity, life and regeneration. Consider the months we spend in the watery cradle of our mother's womb. Warm and protected, we float in the darkness of this soft and liquid hidden world. And, it is with a gush of water that we begin our emergence into the outer world. Is it any wonder that we have such a powerful relationship to water? Our sacred connection with water is innate, with us from the beginning of life.

In art and myth, water symbols include swans, cranes, frogs and dolphins. Spirals, shells, cauldrons and chalices are also used as expressions of the water element. But perhaps the most potent water symbols are the many sacred rivers and holy wells that dot the globe.

Rivers, wells and springs where water emerges from the ground are some of the most honored places on Earth. They are power-filled points where spiritual grace flows, pools and offers itself to us. Around the world, these sources of water are renowned, hallowed places of healing, blessing and prayerful request.

Sacred Rivers

Sailing the Nile, I saw how this river drew people, fed people, and connected people. It is the life-blood of Egypt. This is true of most rivers. And, throughout human history, these great flows of water have inspired culture, legend and religious devotion. We know them by name: Jordan, Mekong, Amazon, Thames, Danube, Mississippi and Euphrates.

Perhaps the most well-known of the sacred rivers is the Ganges. It is a place of death, life, purity and rebirth. Considered a living goddess, her name is Ganga Ma, "Mother Ganges." Hindus believe that anyone who touches these purifying waters is cleansed of all sin. People come to this sacred river to bathe, and ashes of the dead are cast here so Ganga can help them reach the land of the ancestors. Ganga is honored with offerings of grain, garlands of marigolds and pink lotus. Devotees also place small oil lamps and baskets of flowers into the river, set afloat with hope that Ganga Ma will answer their prayer.

Holy Wells

All across the Middle East, Europe, and especially in the British Isles, wells and springs are honored places of pilgrimage. The healthy flow of a well was seen by the ancients as being like milk from the breast of the Earth Mother. Many have flowed without interruption for hundreds of years, never going dry even in times of drought. They are often considered magical, even miraculous.

People come to sacred wells seeking healing from all sorts of ailments and disease, drinking from the well or bathing in the waters to be healed and to receive a blessing. Symbolic of fertility and generative power, wells also attract women who desire to become pregnant. Sometimes water is carried home to be placed on an altar or shrine. Water from a holy well is sprinkled for protection at thresholds, used to cool a fever, or to bless newborn babies. In gratitude, pilgrims often leave a token or votive offering – jewelry, figurines, pebbles and coins are common gifts.

Long ago, wells were seen as an entrance into the womb of the Earth Mother, or a gateway to the Fairy-world or the land of the dead. Many wells were said to have a well-guardian, often a female spirit or goddess. In Ireland, numerous wells were considered sacred to the Celtic Goddess Brigit. The well and the cauldron are two of Brigit's sacred symbols, both reflective of the regenerative, healing nature of water. With the coming of Christianity, many of the holy wells were rededicated with Saint's names. Yet, people's belief in their curative powers did not change.

Many Christian churches and Islamic mosques were built on or near holy wells, with a grotto, garden or other sacred enclosure surrounding the water. At Chartres Cathedral in France, you can still visit the ancient holy well that lies protected in the crypt deep beneath the famous labyrinth there. In Saudi Arabia, the date palm oasis at Al Jawf surrounds such a well, believed to be part of a temple once consecrated to the Sumerian Goddess Ishtar. A mosque now stands on the site and an iron gate guards the well.

There are many beloved holy wells still active today: Chalice Well in Glastonbury and St. Bridget's Well at Rosepark, Ireland; Holywell in Wales; Zamzam spring at the holy city of Mecca, in Saudi Arabia; Our Lady's Grotto at Lourdes, France, and the spring of Meryemana near Ephesus, Turkey. This simple mountain shrine draws Christian and Muslim pilgrims who want to experience the grace of Mother Mary.

Years ago, I visited Meryemana, 'Mother Mary's House.' Legend says this is where the Virgin Mary spent her last years, cared for by St. John. I went to the shrine expecting to find another typical tourist attraction. Yet, as I approached the sacred spring, a deep peace filled me and I clearly felt this was holy ground. As is often the practice at wells and springs, there were bits of fabric tied to nearby tree branches. Pilgrims believe that as the fabric disintegrates over time, so will their illness or concern. Thousands of fabric strips, handkerchiefs and ribbons fluttered in the wind, blurring together in a patchwork quilt of color, each one representing a petition; each one, a prayer to the Blessed Mother.

It was humbling to witness the grief, hope, love and longing expressed at this simple fountain. Prayerfully, I touched the water to my heart and then tied my own tiny piece of fabric next to all the others. Pausing for a moment, I silently asked for Our Lady's guidance and help, and instantly felt an overwhelming sense that I'd been taken under her protection. I felt purified and profoundly blessed.

Whether a spring, a well or a sacred river, I love to visit these holy sites where Sacred Water lives. The experience is always powerful and deeply healing. I am present to the others who have come before me; I sense thousands of supplications, their murmured prayers, heartfelt devotion and desire for divine intervention. And, at the very center of my being, something shifts as I touch the revered liquid with my fingers and use it to anoint my heart, or touch it to the crown of my head. I feel literally showered with grace. I meet a shimmering flow of divine love, pouring down and enfolding me in watery bliss, whispering an invitation to release and gently return to balance.

River of Light

In my adopted home of Thailand, water plays a central role in ritual and culture. The golden Buddha statues are ritually bathed in jasmine-scented holy water. And, at the Thai New Year, people travel back to their home villages to visit the elders of their families, honoring them by sprinkling water on their shoulders as a sign of respect. Water runs deep in Thai traditions, both as a symbol of cleansing and as a symbol of renewal.

Water has a whole season here. During the wet season, the air is heavy and liquid. The smells become rich and damp. It rains heavily, at least once a day. The rivers swell and rice grows in flooded, pond-like fields. Here, frogs, fish and cranes live among the tender, sap-green shoots as they mature into a brilliant emerald cloak that covers the land. In this fertile place Mae Posop, the Rice Goddess, meets her sisters Mae Thorani, the Earth Goddess and Mae Kong Kha, the Mother of Waters. These ancestral deities represent the forces of nature. They are seen as governing the seasons and cycles of life, bestowing abundance.

The end of the rainy season is marked by the festival of Loy Krathong – a joyful lunar celebration dedicated to Mae Kong Kha and honoring the life-giving, bountiful element of water. In one of the festival traditions, people make offerings called "krathongs." Banana leaves are tenderly folded into little boats and filled with flowers, incense, coins and candles. The krathongs are placed in local rivers and streams as gifts to the Mother of the Waters, thanking her for a rich, healthy rice harvest, a symbol of abundance for families, villages and the whole nation. People ask forgiveness for any harm they may have done to the rivers and waters. And, they pray for blessings and continued good fortune.

Our house is very near the river. Mae Ping is her name (Mae means 'mother' – a title given to many rivers). Under a radiant full moon, I watch as people arrive at the river carrying their krathongs – elderly, young, couples, groups of students and whole families together. They reverently light the candles, set fire to the incense sticks, and prayerfully lower their krathong into the river, pushing and splashing to get their little boat out into the current with all the others. Hundreds of krathongs float by, creating a twinkling stream of floating light. It is as if the river is alive with hope and prayers.

Moving to the steps leading down to the waters edge, I light the candle and incense on my own krathong. As I let my offering slip into the river, I whisper my thanks to the water. I ask forgiveness for any way I may have contributed to the pollution of the water. I say a prayer of gratitude for a productive year and I ask for inspiration in my creative life, tenderness in my relationship with my husband, and health for my extended family.

I feel a sense of calm and a wave of happiness lifts my heart as my little boat, such a humble gift, moves into the stream and joins the other krathongs. It is a touching and sweet ceremony; simple, yet so profound.

Sacred Water Within

Let your tears come. Let them water your soul.

—EILEEN MAYHEW, ARTIST

Water is the element that relates to our inner soul-life, our dreams and emotions. In the Soul Coaching program, water guides us to release past hurts, dissolve old patterns and clear emotional clutter. Water teaches us to let our emotions flow without restriction, allowing the intensity of love, passion, sorrow or joy to move over and though us. We learn to find graceful movement from one to another, our emotions becoming like the current of a sacred river. Coming to a place not of holding back, but fully expressing, we are more alive and vital as we experience incredible depths of feeling.

As our emotions overflow and pour forth, we often weep. Humans are the only creatures on Earth who weep, with the whole range of emotion (not just sadness) able to bring us to tears. How often have you been moved to tears by some tender act of kindness or generosity? By love for your child. Or, by the beauty of nature. We say that our tears "spring" or "well up," a reference, I believe, to the sacred water we carry within. Some of the most poignant water symbolism relates to tears.

In her book *Women Who Run with the Wolves,* Clarissa Pinkola Estés writes, "Tears are a river that take you somewhere. Weeping creates a river around the

> **Flow**
>
> *AFFIRMATION: The glory of the universe flows through me!*
>
> It's time to let go. You're entering a period of gracious ease and flow. All is unfolding perfectly and with good timing. Everything is falling into place because you aren't resisting the drift of the great river of life.

boat that carries your soul-life. Tears lift your boat off the rocks, off dry ground, carrying it downriver to someplace new, someplace better."

Tears are a powerful current of sacred water that moves us to a place where we can be renewed. I think this is why folklore is so rich with imagery and stories of tears. Around the world, going back thousands of years, there are legends about tears and the marvelous, almost magical power of weeping to cleanse, heal and create. In mythology from Asia to the Americas, flowers spring up, rivers flood, wounds are healed and wishes are granted by the powerful nature of tears.

In Egypt, the 'Night of the Drop' celebrates how the Goddess Isis creates the annual Nile flood with tears wept for her lost husband, Osiris. In Asia, Kwan Yin, the Goddess of Mercy is depicted holding a slender vase. Stories tell us how she pours out her tears of compassion to heal the earth, soothing all those who are suffering.

Magical tears appear in many of our beloved fairy tales. In the Brother's Grimm story of Rapunzel, her tears heal the eyes of her lover after he is blinded. In their original telling of Cinderella, tears wept after her mother's death cause a magnificent hazel tree to grow. Sitting beneath this enchanted tree, Cinderella's tears are filled with her deepest longings, and hearing her laments, a little white bird throws down to her the things she desires. And, in the German folk tale of The Goose-Girl at the Well, an exiled young princess weeps not tears of water, but jewels and pearls. Gathered and saved by a kind old woman, the wealth of pearly tears provides a good life for the girl.

In plant lore, many healing herbs and flowers have legends telling how they sprang up from where tears have fallen. Asters, violets, heather, vervain and ele-campane all have lore associated with tears. In Greek myth, the Goddess Aphro-dite's tears for her slain lover Adonis turn into roses and she causes anemones to grow where drops of his blood touch the ground. And, medieval legend tells of the Mayflower, or Lily of the Valley that blossomed from Mother Mary's tears as she wept for her son Jesus at the foot of the cross.

Even gemstones carry legends associated with tears. In Norse legend, tears shed by the Goddess Freya melt stone and where her tears creep into the center of the rock, they become gold. Where her tears fall into the sea, they turn to lumps of amber. In Lithuanian legend, Jūratė, a mermaid Goddess of the Sea weeps tears of amber which wash onto shore. And, for the ancient Inca people, "Tears of the Moon" were the silver tears of the goddess Mama-Quilla, Mother Moon.

Another tradition that speaks to the precious nature of tears is the ritual of the tear jar. While visiting the ancient city of Petra in Jordan, I listened as a vendor in a dim, dusty antique shop told me the story of how these slender-necked vessels, called *unguentarium* or *lachrymatory*, are found in ancient Greek, Roman and Nabataean tombs. Some bottles contained precious oils and perfumes. Others held tears. Mourners would collect their tears and bury the jar with their loved one as a symbol of devotion.

Enchanted by this poignant ritual, I bought one of the tiny antique bottles. Its tear-drop shape rested in the palm of my hand perfectly, and the fine terra cotta felt silky smooth. Folding my fingers around it gently, I closed my eyes, visualizing the woman who may have held it so many hundreds of years ago when it was placed in a tomb. I imagined how she held it to her face and poured her tears into it, creating a small well of holy water. The tear jar felt comforting to me. It seemed a vessel of love; a simple receptacle capable of holding a flood of emotion.

Deepening the Connection

> *May what I do flow from me like a river,*
> *no forcing and no holding back,*
> *the way it is with children.*
> *Then in these swelling and ebbing currents,*
> *these deepening tides moving out, returning,*
> *I will sing you as no one ever has,*
> *streaming through widening channels*
> *into the open sea.*

—RAINER MARIA RILKE

As we spend time getting to know and understand the nature of water, we become present to its rhythm and movement, aware of how water dances with the tides and changes with the seasons and the cycles of the moon. Water invites us to embrace the flow of life. It shows us how to be fluid. Receptive. It can help us soothe old hurts and purify emotional pain. And, with a gentle ease, it can carry us to a place of wholeness.

Consider places of your own soul that feel stagnant or dry, thirsty for the nourishing touch of water. Think about any need you have for rejuvenation. And, imagine the ways water might play a role in your spiritual life.

The rituals and traditions of the sacred river and the holy well are as useful to us today as they were to our ancestors. Far more than antiquated customs, these potent water rituals can be adapted to modern life to suit our unique needs and circumstances, bringing all the power of the Divine to us now, when we need it most.

Personal Ritual and Ceremony with Water

For centuries, ceremony has been used to mark life's passages and turning points, celebrate significant events and honor major transitions. Creating form and focus, ceremony initiates a powerful path to healing and water plays a central role.

You don't have to go to the grotto at Lourdes or journey to the Ganges to have a deep, healing experience with the water element. I invite you to explore ways to claim these potent water-centered traditions for yourself and design your own personalized rituals.

Your water ritual doesn't need to be elaborate. It can be as simple as offering a single flower to a river. And, you don't have to travel far to find sacred water. Somewhere nearby is a body of water, a lake, a stream. If you are close enough, go to the ocean's edge. But, to connect with the element of water, even your own bath tub will do.

Creating Your Own Water Ceremony

First, set aside some time alone – at least an hour or two. Begin by taking a few minutes to center yourself. Become still, letting your breathing relax and your thoughts become quiet. Pay attention to your emotions and notice what you are feeling right now, allowing it to be just as it is.

Now, consider the purpose of your water ritual. Ask yourself, what is it that needs healing, releasing, cleansing or blessing? Is there a particular emotion that needs attention? Balancing? Take some time to identify this feeling. Name it. Visualize it. Listen to your heart, open to hearing what your spirit needs right now. Are you feeling called to do a ceremony for your own personal healing? Is your soul craving a purification ritual to release some past trauma or soothe a raw, tender emotion? Or, perhaps you are envisioning an act of thanks for the gift of water on our beautiful, blue planet?

When you know the purpose of your ritual, imagine what it might look like. What form will it take? You could create a lavish, luxurious bath filling the tub with flower petals and fragrant oils to signify renewal and cleansing. You might make a tiny boat of bark or leaves filled with flowers to carry your prayer to the sea. Perhaps there is a gift you'd like to offer to the water? Maybe there is an item you want to throw away or some memory from your past you want to release, asking the water to wash it away. Use your imagination. Feel free to draw on traditions from your childhood or incorporate symbolism from your religious background, or even borrow traditions from other cultures that speak to your heart.

Once you see the form of your ritual clearly in your mind, then begin to prepare yourself. Gather all the things you will need – flowers, candles, special soap, bowls, or other containers. You can put these things in a basket, wrap them in a beautiful piece of fabric, or place them on a special tray.

Write a blessing, prayer or poem to use during your ceremony. I like to hand-write this on beautiful paper and read it during the ritual. You might want to create an altar or offering for the Mother of Water (this could be Mother Mary, Brigit, Kwan Yin or whatever image of the Divine you feel most connected to). Once you have finished your preparations, set a time for your ritual. I like to do water rituals early in the morning or in the evening as the sun is setting. Use your intuition.

When the time is right, go to the water's edge. Just *be* with the water. Ask her what name she goes by. Give her flowers. Send her thanks. See what message she has for you. Once you have met her and feel connected to the Spirit of Water, make your offering or request. Bathe, wash, cry and heal in her flow. Pour out your joys and sorrows and ask for her blessings. Let the element of water shower good things into your life. Let her nourish you. She is bountiful, immense and overflowing in her grace. Give thanks for her gifts, and be receptive as she bestows them on you.

Motherly Love

A few sunsets ago, I brought the river a gift: a floating altar of long grasses, seed pods and tiny red flowers arranged on a large, orange leaf. After I released it into the current, I asked what message the water had to share. The words came, "Tell people to come to me. I will give them healing. I will give them peace." I felt the water would carry away anything I was ready to let go of, purify whatever needed cleansing. Nothing was too large or too small. It was an incredible feeling of abundance and generosity. Standing there, watching the sky turning pink and reflected in the still water, as clusters of water lilies floated by, I felt the presence of a motherly kind of caring, a gentle nurturing. I did, indeed, feel peace.

∽

CORAL MUJAES POLA
Mexico City, Mexico

CORAL MUJAES POLA was born in Mexico City in November, 1984, of Spanish and Lebanese heritage. Since her parents' divorce when she was two years old, Coral has lived in five different countries. She has also studied abroad in several different countries.

She started remembering who she was while living in Spain. Since then, life has taken her on a beautiful journey with the opportunity to study with wonderful teachers such as Denise Linn, Doreen virtue, Joan Ocean, Joseph Soler, Louise Hay, and many more.

Coral loves nutrition, so she took up the study of orthomolecular nutrition while living in Spain. She is currently studying for a degree in Communications.

For information on weight loss and addictions visit Coral's website www.saludbillonaria.usana.com

Coral Mujaes Pola is a certified Soul Coach and can be contacted at www.CoralMujaesPola.com

Soul Talk

CORAL MUJAES POLA

Soul coaching is medicine for the soul.
It has been the one thing that has supported me
and helped me overcome my addictions.

Fear, fear, fear . . . It kept coming up for me in my dreams and in my every-
day life. What was it? What did I have to learn from it? *Fear* is a waste of
your valuable time when you don't know how to work with it, when you are not
listening to the message it has for you. I'm currently in the process of learning
how my experiences with alcohol, food and overcoming the fear they grew in me,
can support my life mission.

I don't remember exactly the first time I ever got wasted. I do remember
not being able to stop afterwards. I started drinking at age seventeen. These
days, some teenagers start drinking at age thirteen or younger. It amazes me
how 'low' we've fallen! I remember always feeling *lonely*, no matter what I did or
who I was with. It was the same whether I was in a room full of people or with
my whole family around. All my life I always had a hole in my heart and a very
strong, deep feeling of loneliness in my soul, and sadness. I was filled with fear
and insecurities.

It felt comfortable to blame my parents for what was happening to me. They
got divorced. I have two male parents, my biological dad who I refer to as my
father and the man who remarried my Mom afterwards. He has supported me
emotionally and financially since I was four years old and I have the honor to call
him Dad. My biological father is an alcoholic; therefore it seemed normal for me
to develop the 'disease.' It really was my best excuse for some time. I felt I had
been a very lonely, misunderstood and unsupported girl. How often we love play-
ing that victim role, simply because it makes us feel momentarily better and we
use that excuse to justify ourselves.

Even though these were my true beliefs, I was able to transform them. This
was only after I cleared my vision and healed my past through past life regression
and Soul Coaching. Before this, my 'victim feeling' was always giving me permis-
sion to be an alcoholic and to succumb to social pressures by becoming a bulimic.
I hung on to alcohol, partying, boyfriends, girlfriends, anything that would make

me feel a little 'less alone' and would help me to avoid facing myself. Of course, alcohol made me feel worse afterwards; my hangovers were just unreal.

But my physical hangovers where not as terrible as my heart and soul hangovers; my emotional world just collapsed. My friends never really understood why after partying I just was unable to sleep like normal people and would feel like I was slowly dying. Seriously. Not to mention the pack of embarrassing things I had done the night before. Huge lagoons where always with me the next day. I wasn't able to remember what I did; everything was a blur. But I could not stop drinking. Imagine how much I was drinking if, within just over one year after I began drinking, I was already in rehab. Yeah that's right, only one year.

Before that my parents, in their desperation, had sent me to Krishnamurti's school in London for one year. They thought this would help me because of the method of teaching there. They never obligate you to do or study anything you don't want to. But my alcoholism only grew worse; I literally don't remember my year in London. I would drink at least three days a week and when I was not drinking I was sleeping. But even before I developed alcoholism in my life I was always feeling lonely. I was angry at my parents and blamed them for my lonely childhood. I felt different from all of my seven brothers and sisters who were all good students and well behaved – a lot to be compared to.

I felt I didn't belong anywhere, like the Ugly Duckling of the family. I didn't like school because I didn't feel supported in the things I liked – sports, dancing, singing and performing, though discipline for me was almost impossible. I was once a good tennis player and gymnast until partying took over. I felt frustrated, scared, alone and insecure in every way; it was really hard growing up for me. I was sent to a boarding school in Switzerland one year at age sixteen and also lived away with my aunt and cousins for two years. My parents hoped that all these experiences would do me some good. I didn't graduate with honors of any kind, just letters from the different school directors complaining about my behavior and threats of kicking me out of school. Surprisingly, I never got kicked out of any school. My angels were working very hard every day!

It was in Switzerland that I became familiar with bulimia. My close friends there where bulimic and taught me to think that food made you fat. But it was only after I started drinking that I started vomiting. It was not easy for me dealing with the pressure of the people around me and a judgmental society which is intolerant of overweight people. No one in my family has drinking problems (besides my biological dad with whom I never lived and barely see) so you can imagine how hard it was being both fat and alcoholic! I was driving my whole family insane, not to mention dyeing my hair, getting body piercings and tattoos. In their frustration they kicked me out of the house several times at all ages. This was a very painful experience; I felt miserable, misunderstood, and I was *lost*, really lost.

Yet my problems did not start at age seventeen. I had always felt different since I was born, and it seemed that in the eyes of everyone I was 'messing up' all the time. In school I was always the rebellious one. Every year my parents were called in to the principal's office more than once. I would cheat, miss school, change my grades on my report card; I was just very naughty and always had big issues with authority. *Fear.* It's such a powerful emotion when you are being consciously or unconsciously controlled or limited by it. I had been in so much pain for most of my life that I had learned how to survive with my secret fears – literally survive – as I unconsciously carried around the heavy weight of negative emotions and painful memories, secrets and secret fears. Most of the time our extra weight goes hand in hand with what we try so hard hold onto – our victim roles. So to lose your extra weight you have to LET GO.

I do love my life, and my past most of all. Though you may find yourself asking, "How can this person love her life living like this?" When you find yourself asking this question remember this . . . that is where magic lies – in my life as well as yours. All of life's challenges come to us with a gift, an experience, wisdom, and a beautiful opportunity to grow and evolve. When these same challenges don't seem to go away 'fully,' it's usually a sign that they contain an unrecognized blessing, and we should pay more attention. I'm not asking you to understand or believe in everything I believe. I'm simply asking you to open your mind.

We ask ourselves whether there is 'something else' out there. We ask if there is a possibility that the divine world and celestial beings of the light and dark exist; and what if they are real? What if just by closing your eyes you are able to change or transform your past, your present, and your fears? How can contemplating these questions shift something inside you within seconds? When I find people, sadly very often young people, who don't really believe in anything, I feel very sad. Because once you get to know that there is more to life than previously imagined, you want everyone to know and acknowledge the right to happiness and abundance that we were all born with.

It's like knowing where free food and water are in a starving world. You definitely want to tell people, especially the people you love, but I have learned that this is something you cannot impose on anyone. It has to be asked for. It's synchronicity; we all have our different times. We are individuals and we have to respect everyone's past and path. People open up to this information when they are ready to mine for their spiritual gold. It doesn't make you a bad person if you have trouble believing this, or just don't at all. We all have our time, and spirituality comes to us only when we are ready, just like everything else in life. But I love to share what I think is valuable information with others, especially when it could transform their life in a positive way.

Soul Coaching for me is the gift that Denise Linn gave me – *the information on how to connect and be aligned with my soul, the Creator within all things; my mission and the power to transform everything in my life.* And it is up to me what I do with it. I always remember this phrase "With great power comes great responsibility." This is what we as Soul Coaches around the world have – a huge responsibility for what has been given to us. What counts is not what we have, but what we can share. And Soul Coaching is for everyone. As a life philosophy, it embodies purity, humility, power, love and service.

It's strange how we equate spirituality with certain activities. Why do we think that only if we do certain things we are spiritual? Spirituality is more than just meditation and silence; it's a state of mind, and a new way of seeing the world. It's having the power to be conscious in all of our everyday activities, and to transform the intention, the reason and the outcome in everything we do, in order to always serve and do good for the people around us and throughout the world. It's very limiting to believe that to be a Soul Coach or *spiritual* you have to live a certain way . . . not get married, have fun, have kids, enjoy your friends . . . you know, the normal activities, or to relate spirituality to certain activities. That's very limited thinking. Although it does requires discipline and persistence.

If you have this book in your hands you are probably already an awakened soul. You are already looking for clues on what the next step is in your evolution, and most importantly, *remembering* who you are and why you are here. Remembering has been my most challenging task. And even thought I now remember that I made my commitments and arranged everything before coming to earth, that I chose this life with the parents I have, the country I was born in, the problems I have faced – in order to have them as support throughout my life, during my time here, to fulfill my mission, as we all do, I still sometimes doubt. But I have a message for you – Doubt and do it anyway!

It all starts when we decide to re-incarnate with the final purpose of becoming throughout our different reincarnations, more and more a channel of support and love for all human beings as a part of our own evolution. We all have different lives and not everyone has the same kind of mission. We are all evolving and as each day passes, speed keeps increasing. Can't you feel it? Just look around you. All the apparent "disasters" are not what they seem. They are nothing but alarm bells awakening more souls. Our world is full of distractions and a code full of human laws where spirituality is not included. We no longer remember who we are and what we are here for, nor have the sensitivity to even believe that we are only 1% visible. It amazes me how much we have forgotten. But we've always had tools around that are whispering to us, trying to help us wake up from this superficial rational world. I don't judge anyone, especially

> ## Acceptance
>
> AFFIRMATION: *I unconditionally accept, cherish and love myself just as I am.*
>
> *Acceptance is a sacred act of power. Accept your light! Embrace all parts of yourself! Allow yourself to receive the gifts of the universe. You're worthy of these blessings and so much more.*

when so far I have lived the majority of my life blinded by my ego and controlled by external distractions, ranging from people to substances. I once was a slave to a simple thing like food.

Waking up is not always hard, but we do need to keep up a daily awareness of what we have learned, and maintain our spiritual discipline. Just like everything, we desire to grow. This too requires maintenance and 'updates.' I won't say it's the easiest thing on earth to do, to wake up and realize how much you think you've wasted or lost. But you haven't really lost anything. All circumstances in our life, regardless of our good or bad labels, have been supporting us all this time, in becoming who we are meant to be. It's just a matter of walking forward, facing our paths instead of walking backwards, being hit by unnecessary things. *Alignment is the key to evolution.* That's what Soul Coaching is. It is our instruction on how to get in contact with our higher self, our soul, and our ancestors.

It's very interesting for me to observe what happens when I stop doing what I know maintains me in 100% happiness and health. I start wanting to do things I know are harmful for me and craving for old things and habits. What keeps me in balance are: meditation, exercise, eating healthy, writing, reading – things that nourish my soul and my intellect in a positive way. When we switch and nourish our body and soul instead of our greed and ego, we automatically no longer crave for 'destructive things.' You don't have to struggle. If you do the things that feed your soul, you won't feel the need to go back to old habits. Soul coaching is for me my medicine, my food, my nourishment. As well as being medicine for the soul, it has been one of the most important things that has supported and helped me overcome my addictions and problems.

Even though Soul Coaching has changed my outlook on life, transformed my addictions and given me light and happiness, I still sometimes get the urge to socialize, to see my old friends, and to behave like a "normal" young person, according to society. I'm only 25, not that old; but I'm not a teenager anymore. The difference is that I am much more aware of things now. I am fully aware of the divine world which gives me even more responsibility for everything I think, speak and do. Maybe you are thinking, "How is behaving like a normal young person in any way wrong?" Well, I was an alcoholic and bulimic for many years, so in human laws if you are an alcoholic and have been treated, you can *never* even smell alcohol again in your life. It switches on a part in your brain that makes you unable to stop drinking.

I am not a doctor or a psychologist, but there are many books available and professionals who specialize in this area. So if you need help, please get it. I am a professional Soul Coach and I believe in truthful communication about life and healing. I respect everyone's point of view but spirituality was the only thing that worked for me and it became the only way I could 'treat myself.' Deep inside, it felt right for me.

Though I may sometimes doubt myself, what's most important for me is that

I am someone who lives in integrity with what I teach, say and actually do, and to truly be a person who lives what she believes. It's not always easy, and my path has not been perfect, but I KEEP WALKING and so shall you. It's true that I've done absolutely everything written in this chapter. Believe me I've walked my talk! Everything here has indeed happened to me, but Soul Coaching's beautiful path has supported me deeply in my healing process. I can't say this and then go off and be someone else in my everyday life. I just cannot do that. It's a universal law. My words would lack power and would have no effect whatsoever on people I serve. Remember, you don't have to be perfect. So be gentle with yourself while you are in this powerful transformation.

Recently I had been in conflict with myself because I was blaming myself for wanting to go out with my friends, etc. It brought up deep fears for me. But life took me to Spain so I could synchronistically re-meet my very first spiritual teacher there. I told him everything that was happening to me regarding my fear of socializing normally with my friends. And with all the calmness in the world he turned to me and said "Integrate it. Don't fight it." Those words resonated in my soul and felt very wise for me. So I did; we did; he helped me. So I have now learned to *integrate* everything I do in a spiritual way. I don't use labels anymore or judge myself if I feel I want to go out and have fun, which if I'm connected and aligned doesn't happen anymore. I'm no longer scared of alcohol or food. They no longer create fear within me. I'm becoming more and more free. I won't say this will work for everyone but I offer this to you as one more option to work with your gifts (addictions or whatever problems you may have).

I do need to tell you that once you awaken your spiritual path, you won't have the urge to be with the same people you were once with, nor go to the places you used to go. There is a strong possibility your friends will change, as your interests change. It happened to me. We just shift our vibration and usually we are attracted to people and friends who vibrate at our same level. Remember there's no good or bad; but as we change, everything around us changes too. Just keep it simple.

Keeping things simple and easy is what has worked for me. In the past, when I've started imagining spectacular things in my mind and wanting to do something beyond my expectations, for some reason I never got them done. But as soon as I start *just doing them*, keeping that empowered feeling for as long as I can, this is when I get everything done that I need to do.

I remember this happening to me in one of Denise's workshops, while making collages and spirit sticks. There were just so many different materials and colors laid out on the table I didn't know where to start. I wanted mine to be just gorgeous and use everything on the table if possible. My imagination seriously can fly very high; I bet yours can too! Shortly afterwards I said to myself "Dude, just take little but meaningful things and you'll do great." And that's what I did. With very few items I created wonderful things, and what's most important is that I finished them both! You see, I had always had issues with getting things done and finishing what I started, with everything from homework to a diet. Many people do this with books as well – let's just get one read and then buy the next one. Multitasking really doesn't work for me, although some people can do it. It is really wise to just take one thing, finish it and then take another one. Otherwise you become dispersed and never complete anything.

I have learned from experience dear reader that keeping everything short, easy and simple always works best!

Aligning with the Soul – Morning Ritual

Always remember that it's crucial how we start our day.

As you know, Soul Coaching has helped me overcome my addictions, or "excesses," as I like to call them. I used to think I could find equilibrium in my multiple excesses. For example, I would eat too much food for several days in a row and then for another several days very little, then exhaust myself over-exercising. I thought "This way, what I gain I will lose." Not true! Excess is excess, whether it is for one time or several days. Don't fight or try to get rid of what you want to change; *replace it* with activities that you like. Exercise for at least 10 minutes each day, but don't overdo it. This has a huge impact on your health and energy because exercise suppresses hunger and cravings.

Check what time of the day you feel more anxious or craving more and try to exercise at that time. Your cravings just mean you have more energy at that particular time that needs to be addressed in a healthy and positive way. You could also use this time for painting, singing, dancing . . . whatever makes your soul smile.

I'd like to share with you my morning ritual for starting the day. These activities fill my soul and my 'empty spaces,' so I don't crave anything destructive. I encourage you to find your own tools in your everyday routine. These activities will be your medicine and support towards your goal, whether it's losing weight, stopping smoking, awakening your consciousness or enhancing a relationship.

As we walk towards realizing our dreams, we each encounter different 'limitations.' But we have the capacity to transcend anything in our life and we really have no limits. It doesn't matter how many times we fall; what matters is how fast we stand up! *Never ever stay down.* Remember, falling down *does not* make us a failure.

Each morning I realign my energies to maintain my equilibrium. I like to wake up early and give thanks. Gratitude is truly the most powerful tool we have, and it's FREE! Waking up early gives me a sense of being able to take advantage of even the first ray of light. If I'm at home in Cuernavaca, I love to go up to my rooftop and watch the sunrise. The sun fills us with energy and love, and cleanses away any harsh energies. It's very important to tune in with the energies of the sun and the moon. As women, the moon supports us with different energies through its four phases.

The New Moon is a good time to begin something new, to seed. The Full Moon is a time to harvest, gather in. When the moon is diminishing, we evaluate and let go of things that no longer support us. The moon affects all the water in our world and creates the high and low tides. Our bodies are made up of 80% water, so the Moon also affects us. By aligning with the moon's cycles, we gain support and strength for our different activities. It's like surfing with a wave . . .

After we wake up, it's very important to clean not only our energy, but our bodies as well. To be in alignment with what we want in our lives, we need to nourish our soul as well as our physical body. Being healthy and nurturing our skin and our cells is just as important as positive thinking, meditation and affirmations!

To nurture our cells, we need nutritional supplements. Unfortunately, eating healthy food is no longer enough for what our body needs. Even if everything we eat is organic, the soil may be damaged due to pesticides and fertilizers, and chickens and cows are often fed or injected with hormones. To counteract this, I take certain health supplements which you can read about on my website.

Before breakfast, I drink a glass of warm water with half a lemon squeezed into it and blended ginger. That's my morning physical cleaner; it cleans all of the digestive system. I like to be completely clean before I go in front of my deities and my sacred space, so I make sure I've brushed my teeth and washed my face. In this way I pay my respects to them and to myself.

I then sit in front of my altar. I highly recommend that you create your own sacred space. It doesn't have to be an altar; it could be anywhere in your house as long as you feel safe and comfortable. I light a candle and burn incense, then close my eyes and breathe consciously before going into deeper meditation. I also love playing mantras, so these are the first sounds my ears hear.

Only you know how long you need to meditate. Sometimes I meditate for an hour or more and sometimes for just 10 minutes. I like to pray, but you can just *be* in silence. Do whatever makes you feel good and empowered. At the end of my meditation, I take out a Soul Coaching Oracle Card. This helps me to clarify the messages I am receiving from my soul.

With this morning ritual I connect to my higher self, to my spirit and my creator. By taking the time at the beginning of each day to align ourselves, we become more in touch with our soul and fill part of our empty spaces. The other part comes when we actually *do* our lovely activities. This supports us in our goals and helps maintain our daily mental, spiritual and physical health and equilibrium.

Beauty

AFFIRMATION: *I am deeply and profoundly beautiful.*

You're beautiful, inside and out. Your sacred inner and outer space are radiant and glorious. No matter what your age, your loveliness is growing. Create outer harmony in your home environment, even in small ways — such as a vase of flowers, a scented candle, or clean windows — and your inner grace will glow.

CHRISTINE SCHREIBSTEIN
Baltimore, Maryland, USA

CHRISTINE SCHREIBSTEIN has always enjoyed looking at the world through "rose-colored glasses" and seeing the brighter side of most events as learning experiences that become venues for growth. She was able to gather even more joy into her life when she reconnected with the angelic realm, a gift that is there for anyone who wishes to open their heart and embrace them. Christine knows that when calling upon the angels for assistance for life's challenges, no matter how big and small, relief comes and joy itself expands beyond expectations. She teaches that when one feels fulfilled with their cup overflowing, Grace does Always Begin Inside and life becomes the glorious journey it is meant to be.

Christine is married to a wonderful guy; has three great adult children, two loving cats, Gabi the infamous goldendoodle, and a demanding horse. Christine currently calls home the Baltimore, Maryland area as well as Chincoteague Island, Virginia.

Christine is a frequent radio guest on *Today's Woman*, on KHTS AM 1220, speaking about angels and the law of attraction. She is also a contributing author of *The Angel Experience*, released May, 2010. Christine writes the *Daily Angel Chatter*, a free service delivered to your email Monday - Saturday. Lastly, Christine was guided to provide an online certification course – Angel Chatter Intuitive. Be sure to check out these offerings and much more at: www.AngelChatter.com

Soul Coaching with the Angels

CHRISTINE SCHREIBSTEIN

Combining Soul Coaching with the angelic realm can be a beautiful and joyous experience, especially during Fire Week.

*S*oul Coaching and angels? Yes indeed! Angels can and do assist in more ways than you can imagine and are aware of. They motivate, protect and adore you as you move through each week of the Soul Coaching program.

Who are the angels and what does the word "angel" mean? The very word *angel* means "Messenger of God." What better ally to have than someone who always has your highest interest and best welfare at heart? Angels can and do appear in a variety of ways: the stereotypical wings, halo and flowing robes, as an average looking human, or even as an animal. It all depends on the situation and in what form you would most likely accept the assistance. For example, if you knew that an angel was standing next to you at this very moment, with wings, halo, and flowing robes, you may be a bit overwhelmed that you are being singled out for this 'special' event. Truth be told, there probably IS an angel standing next to you right now, but they may not let you know of their presence because they do not wish to startle or overwhelm you.

As humans, you tend to forget that angels can be anywhere and everywhere in a moment's notice. They can and do help thousands, even millions simultaneously. This is one of the most important messages to take with you after reading this; you are *never* too unimportant to request their assistance. No project, event or request is too big or too small. So ask away! The angels get very tired of filing their nails, singing and passing away the time waiting for requests from *you!*

Think of moments in your personal life when someone just happened to appear or call when you needed it most. Perhaps you are late for a train or the bus; a total stranger appears and puts your mind at ease and helps you board that train or bus with time to spare. Perhaps you felt uncomfortable in a situation only to have someone, even an animal, appear by your side to calm your fears, allowing you to feel extremely protected. These are moments of angelic intervention, pure and simple. As long as you are willing to ask *and* receive the help you are requesting, angels are there for you at the snap of your fingers or a glimmering thought in your mind.

Though I personally work and play with angels all day long, it still amazes me when I *know* they have stepped in to assist me. Allow me tell you a story of how they assisted in my personal life in a very matter of fact, but special way.

My husband and I were returning from a second honeymoon. My parents had gladly offered to take care of our daughters while we were away. Unfortunately during that time, my dad was called back to work and shortly after returning home, suffered some heart pains. My mother took care of things for us, arranging dear friends to watch over our daughters for the last 24 hours, leaving her to go home to her dearest love, who was now fine, but she still wanted to be by his side and see for herself. Of course we were fine with this, but now felt that we had to get home immediately, just to be sure our girls were safe and to give them a hug. Our boat docked in New York City and we caught a taxi to the train station.

Upon arrival at the station, we saw cars parked two or three deep from the curb with no red caps in sight. The next train was scheduled to leave shortly and the succeeding train was leaving several hours later. We became frantic. We wanted to get home. NOW.

> ### Inspiration
>
> AFFIRMATION: *I am receiving divine inspiration right now.*
>
> *Be open to divine inspiration! You inspire others. Immense creativity, motivation, and energy are expanding in your life.*

We hopped out of the taxi and as I turned around there was a Red Cap, *who was not there a moment ago.* This lovely man escorted us to the ticket counter, smiling and chatting the entire time, putting my mind at ease; I could even feel my shoulders relax. He then waited by the escalator with our luggage while we checked in. Tickets in hand, we raced to him and we all descended to the train platform. He joyfully settled us into our compartment and as we turned to give him a tip, he was gone. Poof! Nowhere to be seen. The platform was completely empty. You tell me. Was this an angel in disguise assisting us?

Angels intercede on your behalf like this every day of your life, some in not so dramatic ways and some in very dramatic ways. The key is to be open to receiving their love and guidance.

As you delve into Fire Week during the 28 days of the Soul Coaching journey, the angelic forces are with you to assist, guide, and keep you safe from the ego, while allowing you to explore with complete joyful abandon the releasement of things, thought processes and mantras that are no longer serving you – with the greatest of ease, security and love.

Archangel Zadkiel can be a wonderful companion during Fire Week, the Week of 'drying out.' If you are not familiar with this angel, you are in for a treat! He governs the crown chakra, which is purple in color; as is his color resonance. Archangel

Zadkiel's specialty is The Violet Flame of Transmutation. Therefore, what this magnificent angel assists you with is transmutation and transformation. Imagine a flame that warms, but does not burn, a flame that is violet in color, a flame with a power so great it transmutes anything unsavory to pure light-hearted energy of the highest level. Wow! Through this transmutation, transformation occurs on all levels, including how you view the world and react to your surroundings.

Allow yourself to take a quiet journey now, into the Violet Flame . . .
Inhale with a deep cleansing breath.
Exhale.
Continuing breathing as you,
Soften your eyes.
Relax your shoulders,
Ease your mind
and Relax.
See a flame before you that is violet, glowing, and radiating.
You now approach the Violet Flame. See it blazing before you, beckoning and welcoming you in complete harmony with your beliefs and desires. As you approach the Violet Flame, you know Archangel Zadkiel is standing by you, protecting you and welcoming you here.
You feel the warmth of the Violet Flame. You feel its security. You feel its tender strength. When you are ready, you then choose to walk into the Violet Flame for ethereal cleansing. Feel the Violet Flame working, melting away the old energies that surround you, dissolving belief patterns that no longer serve you, making your vision, both internal and external, brighter and clearer. While you stand within the Violet Flame, you feel its power and know this is a reflection of your natural loving power. You embrace the feeling of being grounded while standing within the flame.
When you are ready, step out of the Violet Flame. You now feel rejuvenated. You feel lighter. You feel clearer about everything in your life. Solutions seem much easier to attain. Problems are not so large any more. You are at peace. You give thanks. You may wish to rest a while before continuing on with your day. Remember to drink plenty of water to keep hydrated as the releasement process continues.

I hope you enjoyed visiting the Violet Flame! Keep in mind that visiting and partaking of its properties does not have to take hours. If you only have a few moments to spare, gently quiet your mind and allow this transmutation to take place. When you become accustomed to visiting the Violet Flame and its energies, it can take mere moments to visit, transmute and become grounded yet again. This is how quickly the angels can work. In the span of just 30 seconds, they can change your perception and the perception of your world for the better.

You may enjoy visiting the Violet Flame so much you wish to have a tangible object to remind you of the peace, the transmutation and transformation that takes place while there. An amethyst crystal is a perfect choice because it does exactly what the Violet Flame does: it transmutes energies. This is why so many healing centers and metaphysical stores have amethyst geodes as part of their decor. An amethyst crystal continually works on transmuting the energies within the room it is in, clearing the space of unwanted energies while keeping the area sparkling in energy and not requiring much in return. In fact, all that an amethyst requires from you is periodic dusting. It is also one of the easiest crystals to acquire; being available in most metaphysical stores, jewelry stores as well as science museums. You could not ask for a better start in the crystal kingdom for your personal or work collection.

Archangel Michael is another one of the great archangels that can be very beneficial during Fire Week. He is known as the "great protector," and he has been designated as the patron saint of the police force in the United States. Archangel Michael is typically illustrated as dressed in armor, carrying a shield and sword. While the sword is illustrated as metal, in reality the sword he carries is a vibrant blue flame. Michael's sword is often called the "Sword of Truth" because it cuts through the nonsense and gets to the heart of the matter in any situation.

When I initially began working with Archangel Michael, I tended to get very warm. So warm in fact that I found myself pushing up my sleeves even if I was wearing a sleeveless top! We have since come to an agreement and he no longer makes me so warm, but I still know when he is around for I begin to feel expanded, my eyes are clearer and my soul just wants to soar.

How can this great archangel assist you in your daily living? Whenever you feel stuck, in any situation, in life, or even in traffic; ask him to remove all obstacles that are not serving you, in the gentlest of ways. Using words such as "gentle," "loving," and/or "joyful" in your request sets the tone that you wish to have your lessons in a palatable manner. There are times that in your zest for feeling whole again, you may not realize how far you've drifted from your center; therefore, if these obstacles are not removed gently, lovingly or joyfully, you could experience a healing crisis which could lengthen the entire process and certainly make it less than joyful.

"Why don't they hear me and get me out of this traffic?!" Remember, there are times when traffic is preventing you from getting into an accident. There are times you are meant to go slower and enjoy the music, the conversation, the journey (metaphor intended). There are moments when the timing just isn't perfect for you to launch into the next level of your career, romance, etc. Learning to trust in the process is paramount. No micro-managing allowed! Just be assured that whatever you ask for – when you ask truthfully, soulfully and in earnest – is heard and acted upon. This wonderful journey of yours is about staying very present in the now moment and saying "yes" to all that is offered to you. Even though you may not understand exactly how the angels will respond to your request, there is a plan and that plan is ultimately yours and where you desire to be. Allow the angels to assist you in your journey, to introduce you to the people, places and things that launch you to exactly where you truly desire to be. It is a wondrous ride. Enjoy it to the fullest!

Trust in Michael's abilities to cut through the 'yuck' to allow you to be made whole again. Trust in Michael that not only will he cut through all of it for you, but will also assist in the healing process and remind you to stand strong in your power. You see, Archangel Michael governs not only the solar plexus area, but also the throat. He assists you in speaking your truth in the most professional, honest and loving way possible. Just because you stand in your truth doesn't mean you are egotistic! Oh no! By standing in your truth, you become stronger from within. You've learned that you are a vibrant, brilliant, beautiful soul who is meant to be heard, who is meant to be powerful in loving ways, who is meant to be articulate while expressing your truth. Rejoice in this new-found strength. Rejoice in this new-found ability. Rejoice in you!

If you wish to work with Archangel Michael on a more personal level, image yourself being surrounded by a sphere of blue and yellow light. These are his colors: blue for the throat chakra and yellow for the solar plexus. Feel your spine elongate as you feel your inner power expanding. Now place your hands over your solar plexus chakra and feel the strength and the fire from Michael's sword igniting you from within. Sit with this knowledge for as long as you desire. If you wish, place one hand on your throat and let the energies build between the two chakras, allowing your innate power to flow through in all conversations.

If you would like to have a tangible reminder of Archangel Michael's presence, you may wish to obtain some Lapis Lazuli. This stone is extremely helpful for communication in all areas. For example, if you wish to communicate better in writing, first ask Michael, and then place your crystal near your computer keyboard, paper or journal. If you need assistance in drawing, do the same. If you need assistance in speaking, you may wish to carry the crystal in your pocket or purse, or wear it as a piece of jewelry. Call on Michael when you wish assistance in painting, sculpting, pottery or photography as well. Any creative endeavor is an expression of yourself, so calling on Michael and using the lapis lazuli can assist you in feeling more empowered in your creativity. This is why Michael and Lapis Lazuli make such a beautiful combination: the tangible and the spiritual. The Dynamic Duo!

If you would like more assistance in standing strong in your own power while working with Archangel Michael, the following crystals will help. The first is yellow calcite. The calcite family of crystals tends to be softer in nature so if you are feeling rather intimidated by standing in your power, start here. The yellow calcite will initiate the process in a slow, gentle and loving way. Another is yellow apatite. This crystal is a bit stronger in its energy and is recommended for those who wish to move forward more quickly and/or are more self-assured in their presence and just need some extra *oomph*. Enjoy playing with Michael and his associated crystals as your journey is truly meant to be joyful.

The last angel that has come forth to be written about for this glorious book is Archangel Auriel. She is vastly different from Archangels Zadkiel and Michael who are very focused on the Fire element and the qualities of clearing and transmuting. Auriel is focused on your destiny. In fact, one of her names is "Angel of Destiny." Archangel Auriel resonates with the moon and its energies; and just as the moon reflects the sun's energies, Auriel can reflect back to you your truest desires. You can connect with this beautiful angel every night to remind yourself of where it is that you desire to go or be, while at the same time realizing that you are exactly where you are meant to be at this exact moment.

You have learned to transmute and transform areas of your life which then led you to stand strong in your innate power while speaking and expressing your truth. Archangel Auriel is a natural next step. She likes to remind you that our living experience ebbs and flows, just as the moon cycles do. Some days are full and expansive, while others may be a bit more hermit-like. Embracing these living experiences as they present themselves allows you to rest, charge ahead, rejuvenate and move forward with the greatest of ease and grace. Auriel is luminescent in nature and when you truly and purely decide to embrace your destiny, she is by your side, holding your hand while illuminating your path.

Using a moonstone while working with Archangel Auriel is a beautiful way to feel her energies while reminding you to love yourself and allow the day's or life's circumstances to flow over you while standing strong. This luminescent stone, just like Archangel Auriel, has soft energies that remind you of the cycles of life while assisting to keep you on track for your soul's destiny. It supports you in the knowledge that everything is absolutely perfect right *now* and through this acceptance, more joyous, abundant and loving events are certain to follow. Remember if you argue with the process, or play the downside of the 'what if' game, those energies are sure to follow you around. Instead, play the positive side of 'what if.' It's so much more enjoyable and expanding!

For example, you may enjoy animals and wish to work with them. However, becoming a veterinarian may not be plausible for you because your connection is too deep and you feel you would be unable to cope with the sickness that comes with the territory. Take a fork in the road. Auriel can show you other ways to assist animals. Perhaps you could become a professional massage therapist or an acupuncturist for animals, or open your own store catering to specialty foods, toys and gadgets that owners love to purchase for their four-legged family members, or start a charitable organization to sponsor unwanted animals, or perhaps even a certain breed of horses or large cats. The list is endless as you can see. Just ask Archangel Auriel and she can work with you to find the truest and best fit with your soul. All you need to do is ask and then be open for the ideas to come flooding in.

As you delve more into the angelic realm, you begin to realize that blending angels with soul coaching is a wondrous melding of great energies for you and your vision. Now you are better able to pull from this into a more practical endeavor: a vision board!

Why make a vision board? Making a vision board for yourself illuminates what your soul is trying to tell you it desires – therefore, what *you* desire. Before embarking on this quest, ask Archangel Auriel to assist you in finding the right magazines, the perfect phrases and pictures within those magazines and ultimately in helping you to lay them out so they now illuminate to you what is in store for your future. Ask Archangel Michael to empower you so you feel worthy in receiving all that you desire. Ask Archangel Zadkiel to transmute any sabotaging thoughts so you are completely in your own power, embracing all that you are and all that you wish to become. Your board becomes pure joy to behold on a daily basis. This is indeed your destiny. You see, your truest destiny doesn't waver. What does waver is the journey.

As you can see, working with the angelic realm in combination with Soul Coaching can be a beautiful and rewarding experience, especially during Fire Week. The angels are truly some of your best friends. They always have your best interests at heart and can be with you in a moment's notice. There are countless numbers of angels out there to assist you.

You don't have to know the angel's names. They are certainly not offended if you forget or don't know. However, they *are* thrilled to be asked. So ask away and then be open to receiving answers. Then be sure to act upon those answers even if they don't quite make sense. You never know what may happen next. You asked for assistance because the old way didn't help. The angelic realm will help you to think outside the box, so some of their responses may surprise you. But these are often your most valuable solutions. Enjoy the process. Enjoy the dance. Enjoy the journey and don't forget to also enjoy the detours and forks in the road. You may just meet an angel along the way!

Vision Board

A Vision Board enables you to creatively articulate what you desire to have in your life by using photos and phrases from magazines, flyers and even computer-generated images.

The materials:

Poster Board – as large or as small as you feel comfortable working with

Rubber Cement – keeps the paper from getting crinkly

Scissors

Two to three magazines of your choice. Pick magazines that reflect your projected theme. For example, you probably wouldn't need travel magazines if you were focusing on a new home.

Extra, but not necessary materials:
Feathers
Construction or scrap booking paper
Glitter
Beads
Scraps of fabric
Any other decorative material that you would enjoy placing on your Vision Board

Process:
The process of making your Vision Board is meant to be a joyous exploration and articulation of *you*. Therefore, don't start when you are tired, rushed for time or aren't in the right mood. The results will be less than magical and you will have put unwanted energies into your creation.

Grab a favorite beverage, light some candles and put on some music. In other words, set the mood and restate your intentions for what you wish to create within your world. You have already started this process when your magazines were purchased; begin now to leisurely go through them. Look at each page as an individual entity that stands on its own. Phrases may pop up at you – incomplete phrases, phrases that are part of a title or advertising campaign. Try not to judge or think twice; simply rip that page out!

The same goes for photos. The odds of finding a photo in a magazine that looks exactly like beautiful you are rather slim. Just go with how you feel when you look at the photo. Does it make you feel empowered? Does it make you feel healthy? Does it make you feel sexy? Does it make you feel strong? The photo you choose doesn't have to be reflective of your same skin color. It doesn't have to be the same hair color. It doesn't even have to be in the same age bracket. Go with how it makes you feel.

After you have gone through your magazines once, go through them again. You've ripped out pages and the energy has shifted within the magazines and you may see something very important to you that you missed the first time around.

Thirdly, cut out the photos and the phrases as they pertain to your intentions. Use creative-edge scissors or regular scissors. It doesn't matter – it's your board!

Now arrange all of these photos and phrases on your Vision Board. Play with this. Arrange and re-arrange. Remember, all of those photos and phrases may not make it onto the finished board. Don't worry; you may have just needed to be reminded of a certain feeling and can now move on. It's very important that you simply play at this stage. Put phrases over pictures. Layer phrases over phrases to state the exact sentiment you wish to see. You may be surprised how beautifully these random phrases and photos begin to take on a life of their own and how they truly interact and work together. Ahhh . . . doesn't this feel truly divine?

After you are pleased with the placement of everything you have decided to include, out comes your rubber cement! If you have decided to use decorative paper, arrange these directly on the board and glue them into place. Now begin to add your phrases and photos.

Once this is done, feel free to add any other embellishments that you are drawn to add: feathers, business cards, glitter, etc.

Relish in the completion of your beautiful, very personal Vision Board! This is a true reflection of you, your desires and your world. Enjoy looking at your board daily and enjoy the magical effects as they begin to integrate within your daily life.

With great love and joy, I wish you wondrous new beginnings that start with the creation of your Vision Board!

∾

JENNIFER DE VALK
Vancouver Island, BC, Canada

DON'T LET HER comfortable home on peaceful Vancouver Island fool you. Don't let her three beautiful kids and doting husband lure you into a false sense of security. Don't let the two dogs, two cats, two goats and two businesses make you believe she can only handle challenges in pairs.

This girl has camped amidst Indian jungles, hiked Nepalese mountains, been blinded by black-flies in Northern B.C., and given birth at home to three HUGE babies. She has also spent many thousands of hours trying to figure life and people out and is slowly coming to the conclusion that letting go is a big piece of this crazy puzzle.

Jenn attacks life with a blinding intensity, teaches by listening, learns with an open mind and loves with total abandon. Jenn is a student of life and a keeper of sacred dreams.

Her Soul Coaching® Training with Denise Linn and all her amazing fellow SC 33 students was transformational and life changing. Denise has given Jenn and countless people complete love, compassion and knowledge and she is a true blessing to the universe.

Jenn would like to dedicate this chapter to her Mom, who grew her, birthed her, loved her unconditionally and has shown her what true compassion is.

Wish it – Dream it – Do It! Anything is possible!

Contact Jenn at www.TwoBees.ca

ᘓ

My Hearth

JENNIFER DE VALK

*The element of fire has always been with me, challenging me to
move forward in many situations throughout my life.*

There is something extraordinary about sitting on my hearth in front of a
roaring fire and allowing the warmth to seep into every cell in my body. It
can transform me back to the time of our ancestors and the bounty fire bestowed
on them. Fire has been there throughout the ages, providing food, warmth and
a place to nourish the soul.

So it was here by my fireplace, almost a year ago, that I sat with tears in my
eyes, not knowing what my future held. I felt like it was there in front of me but
I just couldn't see it. Naturally I began looking back on the path that had led me
to this spot.

My thoughts went back to a time a few years prior when my husband and I had
decided that it was time to end our tree planting careers and move forward with
something new. Although I loved being outside with the elements and wonderful
people, we both knew it was getting too much for us with the kids, although they
loved it! After some time had passed and many more discussions, we decided to
pursue a long-held desire. So, with three very young children in hand we set off on
our adventure and opened our own café, offering fresh roasted coffee and hand-
made chocolates – two things we were very passionate about! After all, what other
two pleasures are so perfectly matched? A deliciously fresh roasted espresso with a
delectable caramel, hand dipped in dark chocolate can be total ecstasy!

One of the biggest rewards of opening the cafe for me was how much I truly
enjoyed seeing people's souls fill with chocolate and coffee love, as well as my chil-
dren's delight in constantly trying to get their fingers into that *gianormous* bowl
of melted chocolate! Throughout the process of opening and running the store
I look back now and think how much Denise's affirmations would have helped
me. It was and is exciting to have my own store, but at times the pressure was so
huge that I felt like crawling underneath my blankets and never coming out . . .
feeling like I was letting down either my kids or my customers. The affirmation
"I am safe and centered no matter what is occurring around me" has since worked
its magic.

Looking even further back, it seems the element of fire has always been with me, challenging me to move forward with many situations throughout my life. I had always been drawn to Fire, but it wasn't until I gave birth to my three wee children that I had my first conscious and powerful connection with this element. As my first labor progressed into the pushing stage and the beautiful baby's head began to crown, I remembered my sister saying "Jenn, it's like a ring of fire!"

It's true that I felt I was going to spontaneously catch on fire in that moment. Everything that fire represented seemed to be channeling through me – the ability to have trust and faith, risk, creativity, to face my own death, and most of all to listen to myself and know that everything would be alright. Fire, seemingly untouchable, is able to penetrate through me on a direct route to my soul, making me want to give it a huge kiss and declare my love for it.

"I love you!" These words are written over my fire place hearth, the place I've constantly returned to over these past ten years. Who would have thought that when my husband and I built our house and the hearth inside it that this hunk of polished concrete would play such a major part in my life? It is here that I've made my most important life decisions. It is here that I've cried the hardest and it is here that I have sat in complete silence, listening to my soul.

So it was on this hearth that, a year ago, I sat with tears in my eyes, wondering what had happened to my spark and to my marriage. Our spontaneous romantic rendevous seemed to have fallen by the wayside. Those tiny irritating disagreements began to take their place. In all the hard work of taking care of the business and my family, it seemed I had forgotten about the girl who was inspired by people who followed their hearts, and took action of her own. Yet through all the hardships, fun and tears, something has always led me back to this spot on the hearth.

I asked myself through tears "I love making chocolate so why do I feel so sad?" By this time the fire had warmed my back so much that my skin was tingling in pure delight. *Fire was speaking to me.* Feeling comforted and drifting off now, I decided it was time to put my thoughts to bed, along with myself and to see how I felt in the morning.

As if in a dream, the four elements of Air, Water, Earth and Fire are like rooms in a house to be visited one at a time in our imagination . . .

I'm in a huge beautiful room filled with exquisitely clad ballroom dancers feeling completely relaxed. I slowly enter the room looking around, ready to pick my dance partner for the evening. There are four handsome men from which to choose for this next beautiful dance.

In the far left corner we have Air. He's a twenty-something youth with a round face and blonde curly locks. His piercing blue eyes are gazing at the people around him. The aura around Air seems to be so clear that he most likely works on clearing himself of mental clutter on daily basis. As he exchanges glances with his companions it is interesting to see how he evaluates himself and others.

Air is someone who can help us make commitments that make us stronger. He makes plans for following through on projects while waiting for the best time to act. I notice that his beautiful silk tie is lying perfectly straight against his crisp white shirt. He is definitely organized; a person who answers his emails and pays his bills on time, something very appealing to me! I continue to watch Air closely. He's singing out loud and taking deep breaths in between each line of the song: he's communicating his truth.

Just as quickly as my eyes found Air, they now move swiftly over to the other side of the room where my next choice stands – Water. Water is an older and very wise looking gentleman. His face is chiseled ever so perfectly, as though a river has carved its way through his cheek bones. I am drawn to his calm, clean demeanor.

Bearing all the qualities of Water, he is assessing the emotions of the crowd, evaluating the relationships that are appearing before him, listening to see if people are communicating with each other from their hearts, saying the things that they have been afraid to say in the past. He is fully in touch with that inner child of his, and he's no doubt thinking "Who can I have fun with?" He has the same child-like exuberance that I have, the intuition I seek, and he's a remarkable dancer I'm sure.

Sitting down not two feet in front of me I spot my third prospect – Earth. Earth appears to be a cross between David Suzuki and Al Gore. He's a shorter man with thick auburn hair and a tidy clean beard. He's a perfect combination of sophisticate and hippy: a man representing the intrinsic world of nature and the pure essence of health. I overhear him talking to a woman beside him about his new ventures in ballroom dancing and how he is taking action towards a positive future. Interesting.

Earth has learned the secrets of how his physical self can function on this planet we call Earth, in perfect balance. It reminds me how important it is to honor not only our spirit but the bodies in which they reside. Just when it seems that Earth has cast his spell on me, a figure appears in the middle of the dance floor. In that moment I am transfixed into a world beyond this one.

An intense heat envelopes me. Fire, the last of the four elements has arrived. Fire is tall with a long, lean and muscular body. His hair is covered by a red silk bandana with the words "Say Yes To Life" boldly written on the side. Bare-chested, Fire is magnificent and courageous, all rolled up into one special package. Fire is somewhat arrogant but in the most endearing way. He is a person who is able to listen to his inner voice which pushes him to branch out into new directions, to use his creativity to take risks. Fire's inner light shines so brightly I can't help but smile, especially when he turns to me with his hand outstretched. I've found my partner at last. I think Fire and I shall get along just fine . . .

I woke up the next morning after weeping on my hearth with a renewed determination, a very proud member of my new club. Overnight something had come over me. I like to think it was a gang of rowdy fireflies that got into my room and circled around me, most certainly performing a magical induction into a club. The club of "Moving one step closer to knowing what the heck I'm supposed to do in this lifetime!" Yes, it's a long name, but I like it.

I had been told by a friend about Soul Coaching but hadn't given it much thought until this one morning. As usual I crumpled the newspaper, split some kindling and lit that favorite most handsome ballroom dancer friend – Fire. I sat down on the hearth, right where I was the night before and knew what my next step needed to be – Soul Coaching, California. Yes, yes, yes that's it!

From that point on there was really no return for me. In the past, every time someone had called me "the Chocolate Lady," I knew that while chocolate was part of my journey, it wasn't my destiny. I wanted to declare "I am not just a chocolate lady! I am other things too, can't you see?" However, on that morning I moved closer to *knowing*.

One of the biggest lessons I have learned from Soul Coaching is to face my fears. As Denise writes, "a fear named is a fear tamed." That morning I woke up with a feeling of knowing a little more about my direction; I named my fear "Moving forward".

As much as I cherish and am impassioned by the creative process that brings me these many new opportunities, it is with equal passion that I resist moving forward *from* previous life stages. But now I knew it was time for me to step up myself and stop waiting for somebody out there to recognize that I might have potential. I began to see the possibilities of becoming a Soul Coach, someone who gives back, a healer in some way. My fear of letting go could no longer be an excuse. I needed to get off that hearth and start making plans for my trip to California.

During the weeks before my departure south I had no idea if and how I was going to be able to pay for the rest of my tuition. The bit of money I had been counting on to pay needed to be used to buy green coffee beans for our store. Hmmm . . . coffee for our customers, or following my path? The morning the money went out of our account I tried so hard to stay positive. I tried to have faith that in some way this whole Soul Coaching journey would work out for me, that this wasn't just another diversion that would keep me from reaching my goals.

My kids felt my disappointment that morning, but it was difficult to explain my feelings to myself, let alone to them, even though *I love them beyond love*, as I like say. Instead, when my husband came home, all of my frustration and fears were taken out on him as his were on me. I thought my journey had ended, that this was it. Perhaps I was never meant to meet Denise Linn or experience those ten amazing days with fifteen other inspirational women. I blamed everything and everyone for standing in my way. I was devastated and angry and that day, after having a horrible argument with my husband, I threw my wedding ring half way across the soccer field that we'd been standing on.

I thought I might feel some satisfaction after this outburst, that some void in me would be filled because everything had come to a head. But I didn't. In that instant, when I thought I had lost my wedding ring, a ring that symbolized everything my husband and I had worked so hard for with so much love, the building of our relationship, our family, our business, our house, and hundreds of little things that create respect and admiration for each other, I had a pit in my stomach so deep . . . a feeling of indescribable horror at what I'd done.

Immediately I got down on my hands and knees and started searching through each blade of grass for my ring with no luck. I returned later that evening before the sun had set with a toy metal detector that I'd borrowed from one of my son's friends. I walked to the area in the field where I thought the ring would be and turned the machine on. It was malfunctioning. Okay, I couldn't work the darn thing. Trying to control my frustration, I knelt down to try to fix the machine and there was my ring! I kissed it and kissed it and kissed it, shedding tears of relief.

I don't know exactly when it was during those next few days but I received an email out of the blue from Denise's assistant saying that Denise had agreed that I could pay the balance of my tuition for Soul Coaching at a later date. I could not believe that I'd been given another opportunity to go on my journey, even though I seemed to be already well on my way!

My husband and children drove me to the ferry terminal to start the first of many legs of my long trip. We had discussed the possibility of my husband driving down with the kids to pick me up in California at the end of my journey. Though there was little chance of this happening I still hoped with all my being that it would.

I said my goodbyes to each wonderful one of them and walked down the stairs and onto the ramp to board the boat. I felt so scared my breath was taken away. The tears coming down my cheeks were full of every kind of emotion. Just before I boarded the boat, another women passed by me talking on her cell phone. I heard only a few words but those words were very clear. "The gods are looking down on you today." An immediate feeling of peace came over me. I had taken a huge leap of faith and trusted my intuition. I was on my way.

I arrived in Vancouver and took a bus to a Backpackers' boarding house. A tight budget equals interesting travels. Later that evening I took a walk on the water and was passed again by someone, but this time it was a guy on his bike. He whizzing by so fast, yet I was still able to make out a few words as he flew by. "This is meant to be." Finally my fear was starting to subside and faith was taking its place.

After a long night at the hostel chatting with a woman who needed to talk, I left early the next morning to catch a bus and then a train, all 32 hours of it, from Seattle to San Luis Obispo, California – in coach. I spoke with some interesting people on the train and tried to explain where I was going and what I would be learning when I myself wasn't completely sure. I knew I was heading to a magical place to meet an amazing woman, though that was about all I did know for sure.

My train got in exactly 32 hours after my departure. I walked off and breathed in the sweetest smelling air you could imagine. So this is California! I asked for directions to the Youth Hostel and set out on my way, moving closer to my final destination. Feeling lighter with each step, I inhaled the heady fragrance of beautiful orange and lemon trees along the way. Finally the next morning arrived. I packed my bag and slung it on my shoulders and headed out to the meeting place, the place where we would all come together for the first time in this lifetime!

My story ends on that day at Summerhill Ranch, as we all gathered for the first time in the living room of Denise Linn's wonderful home. I found my comfy spot on the floor. I looked around the room and couldn't believe I had made it at last.

My journey here ended as it had begun, in front of a fire. But instead of me sitting on my hearth in front of my fire in my little house on Vancouver Island I was here, watching before me an extraordinary women kneeling in front of her hearth with her fireplace behind her.

All the elements are a part of us, including Fire. Whichever way we envision them – whether we see the elements symbolizing four individual rooms in our house or whether we imagine them to be elegant ballroom dancers whom we get to choose to dance with – they are within us, balancing all parts of our being.

If there is ever a time when you too are struggling with your life as I was, try to take a step back and see all the possibilities before you. There is a way, big or small to see your dreams and goals through to fruition. Believe that you have the ability to fulfill your potential in every way, and you will.

By the way, the four most important people in my life drove down to California to pick me up, just as I had hoped they would with all of my being.

Chocolate Truffle for the Soul

Hmm . . . An activity that will help everyone feel bliss and at one with the universe and themselves? I most definitely think that calls for chocolate!

That Fire element that is ever so vivacious and full deserves a pairing with the ultimate elixir of life, chocolate! Highly recommended to make anyone feel a lift in spirit is a little chocolate and coffee love mixed together.

The following recipe is for a chocolate truffle with a hint of fire that will light up every inch of you. This will fill your spirit with warmth and give you an extra kick to help you move forward on your journey!

    1 ½ lbs of milk or semi sweet chocolate for centers
    1 cup of whipping cream
    1 teaspoon of vanilla
    1 ½ teaspoons of chili oil
    1 lb semi sweet chocolate for dipping

Melt the chocolate at a high temperature in a double broiler; keep stirring. When the chocolate is melted, heat the whipping cream until scalding. Let sit for 3 minutes then add to melted chocolate mixture.

Add in vanilla and chili oil and stir. I like to hand stir but feel free to use an electric mixture. Keep stirring up to one minute, until a smooth texture forms. Do not over stir. One more tip – as you are stirring this mixture, envision your life ahead of you and the steps you will take to take action; listen to your soul every day and embrace the person you are.

Refrigerate until solid and roll into small balls. When you are done rolling the mixture, double broil a good quality 1lb of semi sweet chocolate until it melts. The temperature of the chocolate needs to be around 88 degrees Fahrenheit before you can dip and remember to remove the chocolate off the heat.

Take the truffles you have formed and either hand dip (which I love to do because the feel of the chocolate is

> ### Adventure
>
> AFFIRMATION: *Wonderful new experiences fill my life.*
>
> *Take risks. You're entering new frontiers and a period of expansion. Go beyond self-imposed limitations. Look at the world around you in new and different ways. Something exciting is just around the corner!*

so amazing and it is like meditating) or you can use a truffle dipper – long pointy spears used to stick the truffle onto. Cover the truffle with the chocolate and let dry on parchment paper. You can sprinkle some cocoa powder on top while they are still drying.

You're not finished yet! As your delectable, sweet and spicy truffles are drying, it's time to prepare the perfect cup of coffee to go with them . . . or maybe a glass of red wine . . .

Instructions on the perfect cup of coffee
Take freshly roasted coffee beans of the roast of you're preference and pop them in a coffee grinder. A Burr grinder is preferred as it gives a more consistent grind. These directions are for a French Press which is a wonderful way to brew coffee.

For a six cup press, grind enough coffee for six coffee scoops (1 scoop = two flat tablespoons). As a general rule you can add one flat tablespoon of freshly ground coffee for every three ounces of water.

Boil your water and pour over your grinds in the press. Stir. Let it sit for three minutes and then press the coffee.

Your perfect cup of coffee is born! Top it off with your Sweet and Spicy truffle and it is time to sit back and have all your senses consumed.

Enjoy filling your body with the heat of the truffle and remember to listen to your soul a little bit every day. Honor your truth!

∽

MICHELLE CHANT
Canberra, Australia

A CORPORATE GAL by day, a hippy chick by night, Michelle indulges a creative soul through writing, coaching and shaking her chakras!

Committed to bringing balance and depth to her clients' lives, Michelle believes everyone deserves to live deeply satisfying lives that are fun, enriching, creative and full of abundance. Working with people of all ages, Michelle aims to help them rediscover the sacredness of their lives, and to discover their true life's purpose.

A Certified Soul Coach, Dream Coach, and Chakradance™ practitioner, Michelle's diverse background spans the corporate world, complementary therapies and coaching. Michelle is also a member of the International Institute of Complementary Therapists.

And with over 25 years in marketing, Michelle also empowers spiritual and wellness practitioners by coaching them to take control and grow their business through a specialised marketing program she has developed.

Committed to her ever-unfolding evolution, Michelle is grateful to find her own way in the world, and shares her passion with others whose intent is to reach similar goals. Contact Michelle at Michelle@theSoulCoach.com.au or www.TheSoulCoach.com.au

Feel the Rhythm of Your Soul

MICHELLE CHANT

Combining Soul Coaching with the work of Chakradance™
was a natural evolution for me. Both are intrinsically woven
in the work of the Soul.

*O*ften we try to be the person others perceive, or even want us to be, rather than remaining true to ourselves. I have spent many years aspiring to be the person who I thought others would accept and love, only to discover that this 'person' was only a shell, and I didn't know how to be her.

I was exhausted.

It was only after I had a serious health scare that I threw caution to the wind and decided to get to know the real me. This is probably one of the most confrontational things I've ever done in my life: taking a good, long, hard look at oneself isn't a walk in the park.

I was a workaholic – I worked incredibly long hours, yet something was missing in my life. After years of defining myself as 'Michelle the marketing manager,' I wondered who 'Michelle the human being' was, and why I had abandoned her.

After I looked beyond the superficial and began to look deeper, I discovered a soulful woman; she had compassion, strength and a wacky sense of humor.

I found that I drew people to me with whom I felt comfortable and for the first time in my life I didn't feel like an outsider.

So the question is: How do we stop being who we aren't?

How can we shed the mask of the people-pleaser, and the obsessive need for acceptance and love? And how do we escape from that corset of self-doubt and negative self-talk that keeps us so inhibited?

Finding *me* wasn't easy – in fact, it was rather messy. I made mistakes, and experienced disappointments and failure. I read and researched and engaged in endless conversations with my friends, even losing some along the way to betrayal and ignorance.

Perhaps one of the hardest lessons I had to learn was the fact that it is in many people's best interest for you *not* to find yourself.

As I sat at my laptop today and contemplated writing this, I turned the page on my desk calendar to see this quote:

However rare true love is,
true friendship is rarer.

—LA ROCHEFOUCAULD

The last couple of years have seen the close of a few of my friendships, some I thought were in my life forever.

But as I've walked my spiritual path, some friends have joined me, while others have fallen away – threatened by the unknown or unfamiliar; I couldn't say.

At first, I was hurt and confused, wondering if I had done something to offend. But soon I realized that I'd reached a fork in the road, and that I'd taken one direction and some of my 'friends' had taken another.

In my search for love and acceptance, I had become the perpetual rescuer. Add this to my workaholic tendencies and I was displaying all the negative attributes of the solar plexus archetype – *the servant* – the diligent and dedicated worker who focuses closely on details, works quite thoroughly, and serves others well to *their* satisfaction.

I was also very good at giving my power away: when a friend got into trouble or needed help, I would make them my responsibility – I enabled and covered for a friend who was an alcoholic; took the victim of the office bully under my wing to work with them on their self-esteem issues; and I even went as far to employ a friend when she couldn't find work and support herself.

While it wasn't wrong for me to show compassion and understanding towards these people, it was wrong for me to take over their lives and to treat them like victims. What I was doing wasn't empowering them, it was disempowering them. I thought I was helping them, but I wasn't.

Boy, did I make some mistakes.

What I did learn, however, is that you have to make mistakes to find out not only who you are, but who you are not.

My journey in search of 'spiritual enlightenment' began years ago when I immersed myself in the world of the Goddess. As I had lost touch with the essence of me, I needed to reconnect with my inner-feminine. I studied the goddess archetypes, read their stories and tried to apply their teachings to my everyday life.

Each day, when confronted with life's challenges, I would ask myself: "What would the Goddess do?" Now that's a great question but what I should have been asking myself is: "What would I do?" I realized that by asking what the goddess would do, I was still trying to be someone who I was not, and not embracing my inner-Michelle.

So that's when I turned a page in my life, and began to live my life more consciously. I started to listen to myself, rather than everyone else; I began to trust my instincts. Everything in my life went under the microscope: my core values, my workaholic work ethic, my choice of friends, and even the values of those closest to me.

I found a life coach to work with, who shared the same values as I did. She came at things from a spiritual perspective and challenged me in ways that at times made me squirm and want to crawl under my bed and stay there. She pushed me to my limits, helping me to discover my shadow self – you know, that part of yourself that you deny or suppress because it makes you uncomfortable or afraid.

Before long, I started to study the chakras, and ultimately the teachings of Swiss psychologist, Carl Jung. The more I read, the more I delved into learning about my shadow self.

Now we all have a shadow, and a confrontation with the shadow self is essential for self awareness. So, we can't learn about ourselves if we don't learn about our shadow, otherwise we end up attracting it, mirrored back at us by those around us.

I am very fond of an adage from the alchemists of ancient times: *As above, so below, as within, so without, so that the miracle of the one can be established.* This means that what is within us is also outside of us, that inner states of consciousness are reflected in our daily lives time and time again. However, if we are willing to look at the significance of these repeating patterns, we will see the synchronicity of the events and situations in our lives and ultimately begin to become one with ourselves.

It was soon after this, that Chakradance™ found me. I would like to say that I found Chakradance™, but it was more like the Universe clubbing me over the head insisting that I not only experience this dynamic, moving meditation, but become a practitioner in order to teach others.

The purpose of Chakradance™ is to help bring your Soul more fully to life.

The seven major chakras are the energetic gateways through which body, mind and spirit come together, literally embodying the Soul. Using spontaneous dance, creativity and your imagination, Chakradance™ leads to an awakening: a discovery of your true self. But on a deeper level, it is also about healing and balance.

I discovered that by surrendering to the music of each chakra, I could dance from the inside out: awakening and healing ancient hurts, expressing long-blocked emotions, and opening myself up to higher levels of spiritual connection that I thought possible.

Observing not only the changes in myself, but the breakthroughs some of my students were experiencing, I probed even deeper into the Chakras and the teachings of Carl Jung. But I wanted more.

With a knack for helping people to uncover what they're good at, the next logical step was to become a life coach. So I researched numerous life coaching courses, but nothing resonated with me. It wasn't too long before I stumbled onto Denise Linn's website and discovered Soul Coaching, and the realization that my calling was to ultimately help others to rediscover the sacredness of their own lives.

This is when I began to come into myself fully, in all my perfectly imperfect glory. I learnt I had to let go of who I thought I should be, and shed the perceptions others had of me, in order to uncover the woman within. Combining Soul

Coaching with the work of the chakras and Chakradance™ was a natural evolution. To me, both are intrinsically woven in the work of the Soul.

Having your chakras balanced is important. Open and balanced chakras allow your life energy to flow naturally. To maintain balance, there are a variety of healthy actions you can take to help keep your chakras open and functioning properly.

The Root Chakra: Building Strong Foundations

Located at the base of the spine, the root chakra forms the foundation of the chakra system. It represents the earth element, and is related to our survival instincts, to our sense of grounding, our connection to our bodies and the physical plane. It is also related to our health, vitality, prosperity and security.

Healing strategy:
- reconnect with the body
- physical activity
- massage

Gail's story:

Gail is a single Mum who was doing life tough. Before becoming a mother, Gail had been a graphic designer, but had spiraled into depression after her husband tragically died before the birth of their child. Alone in the world, Gail felt she had lost everything.

One day Gail decided to come to a Chakradance™ workshop to escape the worries of her everyday life. During the tribal beats of the earth dance, Gail was overcome with emotion. She realized that she had lost her sense of grounding to life – that her survival, and that of her 11 year-old child, felt threatened.

Surprised by the intensity of these feelings, Gail came to other workshops, and started to notice negative patterns that kept emerging in her life. Before long she approached me about the 28-day Soul Coaching program, where she could explore her feelings and emotions and uncover the triggers for the negative patterns in her life. Gail threw herself into the daily exercises and she was amazed at the insights that were unveiled. Perhaps the most empowering Soul Coaching tool for Gail was the weekly Soul Journeys, where she learnt to connect with her guides and to listen to their messages.

Making ends meet by living on welfare and the odd job here and there, Gail thought the idea of reviving her graphic design career again was beyond her – she'd been out of that world for too long. However, over the course of the Soul Coaching program, I witnessed Gail becoming stronger and more self-assured. She stopped viewing life as a 'victim' and regained control of her life. Before long, Gail enrolled in a graphic design course to update her skills, and got work experience at a local graphic design company. Four months later, Gail is working as a graphic designer for a government department where she has work-life balance, flexibility and job security.

The Sacral Chakra: Reconnecting with the Inner-Feminine

The sacral chakra, located in the belly, is related to the water element, to our emotions and sexuality. It connects us to our feelings and emotions, desires, sensations, and creativity. This chakra brings us fluidity and grace, depth of feeling, sexual fulfillment and the ability to accept change.

Healing strategy:
• movement
• emotional release or containment as appropriate
• healthy pleasures

Teagan's story:
Teagan has been divorced for a few years now and started Chakradance™ to try to reconnect with herself. After a messy divorce, she'd shut herself off emotionally, and the fall-out of this was now impacting every aspect of her life.

She loved the freedom that Chakradance™ offered – to let her hair down and dance with wild abandon, reconnecting with those aspects of herself that she'd long buried. So when Teagan decided to commence the Soul Coaching program it came as no surprise.

In the beginning, she raged against the 'structure' of the program – she made excuses for not doing the exercises. I smiled, didn't judge her and asked her why she thought she was resisting them so strongly. After a moment's reflection she said: ". . . this is hard stuff – I really have to take a good, long hard look at myself and that's very confronting."

One of the issues Teagan wanted to address with Soul Coaching was her inability to trust men – she had built up a wall of protection around her, and wasn't letting anyone in for fear of getting hurt.

The first time Teagan experienced a Past Life Journey, it was a revelation. I took her back to the life where she first developed a mistrust of men. She was transported back a couple of hundred years to Spain. As a young teenage girl, her father had sold her to a bordello where she lost her innocence, and learnt not to trust. As we explored that life, she was sold into marriage to a man who adored her. However, she never relaxed enough to trust this man and led a miserable life.

As we reached the end of exploring that life, I asked her if she'd do anything differently. We wound back time to the point in her life where she was sold into marriage. I asked her to pay attention to the way her husband treated her . . . how he adored her. Spending some time exploring her feelings, Teagan was able to change the outcome to trusting her husband and to start embracing her life.

Eight months later, Teagan is still single, but she is softer and more relaxed. We caught up for a coffee and she told me that she believes her soul mate is just around the corner, and she is looking forward to meeting and building a life with him.

The Solar Plexus Chakra – Embracing our Inner-Power

The solar plexus chakra is the power chakra and is located in the solar plexus between our sternum and navel. It is related to the element of fire and rules our personal power, self-esteem and self-worth, as well as our metabolism. When healthy, this chakra brings us energy and can direct the full force of our intention toward our dreams and goals.

Healing Strategy:
* deep relaxation (stress control)
* vigorous exercise

Leanne's story:
Leanne was an intelligence analyst for a large government department. After coming back from a posting in a remote location, she was feeling lost. She'd seen enough of the seedy side of life and wanted to find a new direction where she could embrace her true-self.

Now Leanne had been to a few Chakradance™ workshops and was enjoying self-exploration through energizing and harmonizing the chakras. When she decided to pursue the 28 day Soul Coaching program, Leanne told me that she tended to always follow the advice of others, believing that they had the answers. She didn't have the confidence to listen to her own intuition.

At first she thought it was just another 'this is what you should do' program – however it wasn't long before she discovered that the program allows you to find your own answers and to begin to trust yourself. Leanne connected with herself at a deep level and began to notice the synchronicities in her everyday life. Her Soul and Past Life Journeys left her feeling invigorated and empowered. Animal totems were entering her life every day with messages for her.

> **Freedom**
>
> AFFIRMATION: *Boundless freedom surges through me.*
>
> *Break free, express yourself, and let your spirit fly! Flaunt your stuff, dance, laugh, explore, and go beyond predictable behavior. Be daring. Fling your arms to the heavens in joy.*

Towards the end of the program, Leanne announced she was pursuing a new career path. She had taken leave from her job to pursue studies in Feng Shui. Today, Leanne is a different person – she is living her truth, trusting her intuition and following her own path.

The Heart Chakra – Feel the Love of your Heart

The heart chakra is the bridge between the lower and the upper chakras, and is located at the center of our chest. It is related to the element of air and is the integrator of opposites in the psyche: mind and body, male and female, persona and shadow, ego and unity. A healthy fourth chakra allows us to love deeply, feel compassion, have a deep sense of peace and centeredness, not only for others, but for ourselves. Love is the essence of life. It is the ultimate healer, the most potent teacher and the inspiration for great works.

Healing Strategy:
• breathwork
• psychotherapy (for relationship issues, grief, self-acceptance)

Rachel's story:
Rachel had it all: a man who loved her wildly, a happy child and a great job. Life was good, that is until she found out her husband had been having an affair for over two years. She was devastated and felt as though her world was crashing around her.

Rachel came to Soul Coaching resigned that she would be getting a divorce. She embraced her weekly Soul Journeys and quickly bonded with her master guide and two animal guides. Every week a discussion would ensue – her guides challenging her every thought and decision.

The daily activities also appeared to lift Rachel's spirit and she found creating a vision board and spirit stick so enjoyable, she made them a family activity. Not long after, I noticed Rachel's attitude change – she was reconnecting with her husband. They were talking again, truly talking about the problems in their marriage, where their lives were going, and what they wanted from life.

Rachel has since told me that she is now more in love with her husband than she has ever been. She has forgiven him and probably more importantly, she has forgiven herself. Today, they are working on their relationship together, reigniting their passion for each other. And to stay in touch with herself, Rachel is now coming to regular Chakradance™ workshops.

I caught up with Rachel the other day and asked her how it was all going. A huge grin lit up her face as she explained: "I may have finished my 28 day program, but I'll never finish Soul Coaching . . . my Soul is forever."

The Throat Chakra – Finding your Truth and Creativity

This chakra is located in the centre of the throat cavity and is related to communication and creativity. The element associated with the throat chakra is ether. Sound, vibration, rhythm, music, voice, words and communication are all aspects of the throat chakra, which is about opening the voice, speaking your truth and freeing your creativity. It is where you take the will from the solar plexus chakra, add it to the breath in the heart chakra and energize the ideas coming down from the mind to express yourself in the world. To open the fifth chakra is to *commune,* a word which forms the root of communication and literally means to be one with. To communicate with self and spirit is to take yet another step toward the realization of unity.

Healing Strategy:
- singing and/or chanting
- non-goal oriented creativity
- journal writing

The healing power of song:
How often do you find yourself singing along with your favorite songs?

Singing allows your voice to become free: your mind relaxes, your suppressed emotions begin to thaw and your spirit has a direct vehicle for expression. The voice is also a direct expression of power. Your energy transforms. You feel it, and everyone else around you feels it also. It's a deep, loving, confidence, which everyone has within themselves, but most people block.

While you are singing, emotions release and you can experience healing. Singing is a powerful way to find joy in your everyday life and to free your body, mind and spirit.

So sign up for singing lessons, join a choir, head out for a night of karaoke, or be really daring and next time a favorite song comes on the car radio, open the window, crank up the volume and sing your heart out!

The Third Eye Chakra
The third eye chakra is related to the act of seeing, both physically and intuitively, and encompasses all the elements. It opens our psychic abilities and our understanding of archetypal levels. When healthy it allows us to see clearly, in effect, letting us 'see the big picture.' To enter this chakra is to discover a world of indescribable beauty. It is to seek the light of consciousness and learn how to focus that light in order to see clearly.

Healing Strategy:
- guided visualizations
- dream work
- creating visual art
- meditation
- colour and art therapy

The Crown Chakra
The crown chakra relates to consciousness as pure awareness and like the third eye chakra, encompasses all of the elements. It is our connection to spirituality, and

when developed, this chakra brings knowledge, wisdom, understanding, spiritual connection and bliss. In our work in the seventh chakra we seek to free our consciousness from its usual distractions.

Healing Strategy:
• meditation
• psychotherapy (examining belief systems)

Feel the rhythm of your Soul
The Greek philosopher Plato once said: *Music and rhythm find their way into the secret places of the soul.*

Music has always had the power to move us in deeply personal ways: it can bring us comfort or move us to tears; it can stir up excitement, faith and joy and it can make us feel more connected to the world around us.

In Chakradance™, the dance of the crown chakra is a devotional dance – a dancing prayer.

Cultures from every continent have embraced some form of religious or spiritual dancing. In ancient Shamanic practice, dance was used to commune with the Spirits, whilst in Ancient Egypt, certain ritual dances were crucial to the successful outcome of religious rites. The Tantric Buddhists of Nepal have an ancient dance traditionally known as *Charya Nritya*, a Sanskrit term meaning 'dance as a spiritual discipline.'

In the Dance of the Soul we open the gateway to the soul through a meditative sacred dance.

If you can't find a Chakradance™ near you (www.chakradance.com), find some music that connects you with your spirituality. Turn the volume up, and allow the music to wash over you, clearing your mind. Imagine a thousand-petalled lotus sitting on your crown chakra and feel it gently opening. Allow your body to move in a dancing prayer to connect you with your creator and feel the rhythm of your soul.

If you are feeling frightened about what comes next – don't. Embrace the uncertainty, and allow it to take you on a journey. Be brave as it challenges your soul, your heart and your mind as you create your own path towards happiness. Don't waste time with regret – live each day as if it's a privilege, not a birth right.

Spring wildly and with joy into your next action. Enjoy the present, each moment as it comes, because you will never get another quite like it. And if you should ever find yourself lost, simply take a breath and start over. Retrace your steps and go back to the purest place in your heart . . . where your hope lives. You will find your way again.

When you stand in your power, trusting your intuition to guide you in making the right choices and decisions for your life, you'll feel inspired and passionate about life.

Weaving Soul Coaching, soul and past life journeys, and Chakradance™, has helped many people to awaken and discover their true self – reconnecting them with the sacredness of their own lives, to live their truth and follow their bliss!

Bibliography

Judith, Anodea. *Chakra Balancing.* Sounds True, 2003.

Southgate, Natalie & Channing, Douglas. *Chakradance: Rhythm for your Soul.* Hay House, 2008.

Joy

*AFFIRMATION: Joy and ecstasy flow
through me wildly and freely.*

*Celebrate and have fun! Embrace life,
yourself, and others. Say Yes! Soar to
the clouds and let your doubts dissolve.
All is well.*

MARIA CLARK

Cape Cod, Massachusetts, USA

INSPIRED IDEAS is the product of Maria Clark's spiritual journey. As a young child, she intuitively sensed what people were thinking or feeling in her presence. As she grew older, often her friends would confide in her and ask for her advice on a variety of different topics. In her twenties, a type "A" personality, she worked a hectic job as a corporate travel manager in New York City. In her thirties and forties, she ran two businesses while raising two small children, leaving her little time for anything else. Maria's intuitive skills seemed to take a back seat to the rest of her life with the exception of the persistent appearance of precognitive dreams. These dreams seemed to reflect inner truths wanting to surface. She began to consciously reconnect with this inner wisdom four years ago after moving from her home of twenty years in New Jersey to Cape Cod, Massachusetts.

In this new life, Maria has once again taken on the role of intuitive counselor. As a Soul Coach, Akashic Record Consultant and Wish™ Game Facilitator (www.thewish8.com), she integrates the interpersonal skills and practical knowledge gained through many years as a corporate executive, entrepreneur, nonprofit advocate and mother of two to offer her clients powerful Soul Coaching® sessions. These sessions help clients remove blocks that keep them from being present in their daily lives, and empower them to connect to their happiest life.

Contact Maria at InspiredIdeas@comcast.net or go to www.Inspired Ideas.me

⨎

As Grace Unfolds

MARIA CLARK

*As the whispers grew louder, I began to understand that with surrender,
grace begins to unfold.*

*I*n my thirties and forties, I began to experience precognitive dreams: a dream that typically involves a perception or knowing of an event before it actually occurs. Like many women of that age, my busy daily life precluded me from noticing the synchronicities that were present, offering silent guidance. One such guidance was a recurring dream that had me moving from my home of twenty years in Bernardsville, New Jersey.

In this dream I found myself seated in the passenger seat of my SUV which was loaded to capacity with many of the belongings that I had accumulated over the last twenty years. As we began pulling down the driveway, I remember clearly looking back at the house with tears running down my cheeks and having a sense of profound sadness. Even though this dream occurred regularly for over three years, I dismissed it as nonsense as I had no intention of moving from the home and community I so dearly loved.

Seven Flintlock Court held all of the memories of my children, cherished get-togethers with family and friends, and the energy of all of my creative endeavors. In essence, it was me. Or so I thought. Ironically, the last time that I had this dream was the night before we moved to Cape Cod. Heading down the driveway, SUV packed with many of our possessions, tears streaming down my face, I wondered how this recurring dream had manifested into reality.

What I did not understand at the time was that on a subconscious level this dream would foreshadow the enormous changes that would occur in my life as a result of this move which took me from my home in Bernardsville, New Jersey to the beautiful shores of Cape Cod, Massachusetts. This move would be the catalyst to launch me forward into an amazing awakening of my spiritual self. I was on fire, burning from the inside out. It would be some time before I could put out the flames.

This spiritual awakening was precipitated by the complete and total breakdown of my physical, emotional and mental bodies. Concurrent with my move, I was forced to deal with the emotional baggage of a mother suffering from dementia, my new status as an empty nester, and the loss of the daily interaction with my good friends that I had left behind in New Jersey. This transition played itself out physically with a multitude of ailments that included severe allergies, acute body aches, vertigo, loss of memory, numbness of limbs, a chronic stiff neck and depleted adrenal glands. I also suffered from depression and extreme anxiety. All of these symptoms were exacerbated by the intensification of my menopausal state.

In the *Wisdom of Menopause,* Dr. Christiane Northrup tells us that the first half of our cycles is a time when we are one or something outside of ourselves, but in the second half of our cycles we prepare to give birth to nothing less than ourselves. She tells us that during this time the more intuitive parts of our brain become activated, giving us feedback and guidance about the state of our inner self. Retrospectively, I now know that for me it was necessary to clear and cleanse my mental, emotional and physical bodies in order to connect to my most authentic self. I had to face my fears on a grand scale. As often happens with fire, the landscape is completely cleared to allow for new and more expansive growth.

Fearful that I would not recover from my illness, I headed back to the roots of my faith, the Catholic Church. I was convinced that somewhere inside the walls of St. Patrick's Church, I would find my salvation. Week after week, I headed back to church, praying to God to heal me. I promised God that if whatever was wrong with me could be healed, I would do whatever was asked of me. In the end interestingly I did not find my answers in the doctrines of Catholicism, but rather in learning to trust and surrender to a higher power. Surrender can be a slippery slope.

As I learned to trust the intuitive guidance telling me that all I needed to know was already present in my life, I began to relate to my faith in a completely different way. I recognized the truth of what I had told my own children for years which was that faith has nothing to do with the physical structure of the church. Rather, our faith is contained within each and every one of us and is reflected in the way we treat others and in the way we treat ourselves. As we connect to that place of love in the center of our hearts, we connect with God. What became clear to me is that when we surrender to a state of grace, intuition becomes a natural state of consciousness. This discovery did not come easily for me, but when it did, it was quite the revelation.

After an exhausting eight months of doctors' visits, with no relief from my symptoms and no apparent diagnosis other than a slightly elevated autoimmune level, I felt that my body had betrayed me. I had hit rock bottom when seemingly from out of nowhere fate intervened with a referral to Dr. Patricia Fater. Dr. Patty is a remarkably caring and kind physician who has a wonderful way of making you feel as if you are her only patient. She exudes a calm and confident energy that is contagious. After thirty minutes of patiently listening to my list of ailments and problems and reviewing my chart, she looked me in the eye and said, "Maria, there is nothing your body can't heal by itself if you believe it to be so." At that moment, it was as if time stood still and in the stillness I knew without any doubt that with a little trust and a little patience I would get better. I left Dr. Fater's office and decided to put my newly acquired faith to the test. I began to proactively regain my health through a serious introspective healing of mind, body and soul.

After about a year, all of my symptoms began to disappear. Ironically, all of the incredible holistic practitioners and healers that assisted me were women who while taking me through this journey, became my spiritual sisters and teachers as well. After recovering my mental, physical and emotional self, I began to get a glimpse of my spiritual being. I am reminded of Dr. Borysenko's story of Natalie in *A Woman's Journey to God* in which Natalie captured my exact feelings as she wrote in her journal:

And now, in my own stillness, I hear something. 'Where have you been?' my inside body whispers to my outside one. Its sense of outrage is present, but dulled by the grief of abandonment. 'I had ideas. There were things to do. Where did you go?' What can I answer? Oh, I had some errands to run. I had a few things to do. I needed to get married and have a child and go underground for twenty-five years, be pleasantly suffocated. I meant to come back. But the bread crumbs got blown away.

For the first time in my adult life, in this place of stillness, I was truly beginning to hear the whispers of what might be possible as I began to trust the inner guidance synchronistically presenting itself to me.

Two years ago, symptom free, I had another dream. Not surprisingly, this dream involved me standing in the middle of the incredibly beautiful kitchen of my New Jersey home in which I had spent so many years cooking, entertaining and nurturing my family and friends. In the dream, my children by my side, the floor tiles suddenly began to crack all around me and the whole house began to shake until it collapsed inward on to itself. I was now suspended with my children above the house. Next I saw my landscaper filling the now large hole with mulch. I remember in my dream telling my children to call their father at work and tell him to make the landscaper stop, as it must be a mistake. Ironically, it had been my husband's decision to make the move to Cape Cod. I woke up from this dream in a very emotional state, angry at my husband and angry at the world.

I was in mourning, for what I did not know exactly.

Melodie Beattie tells us in *The Language of Letting Go* that, "Letting go is a spiritual, emotional, mental and physical process, a sometimes mysterious metaphysical process of releasing to God and the universe that which we are clinging to so tightly." One morning several weeks later, drained of all emotions and for no apparent reason, I surrendered to a peaceful state of bliss intuitively knowing that it was time to move on. It was time to move on from the safety of everything that I knew to be true, everything that defined me; including my home of twenty years, my children, my business, my friends and most of all my community. I was headed toward the great unknown, wiping the slate clean, giving in to something larger than myself.

As the whispers grew louder, I began to understand that with surrender, grace begins to unfold.

Grace is the freely given, unmerited favor of God.
To live our soul's longing is to be willing to live grace filled moments.
To dance, to move gracefully, to receive the grace-filled moments every
day, we have to know that we are worthy not because of our hard work
or our suffering or our eagerness to be other than we are;
we are worthy by our very nature – the same nature that
creates and sustains all that is.

—ORIAH

For so many years, I was so caught up in the act of doing that I had forgotten how to be. As I transitioned into a new life, guided no longer by the pretense of what was acceptable, what looked good, or what was familiar, I began to hear the truth of what my soul had so desperately been trying to tell me for so many years: "Who I am is enough."

With my illness behind me and a renewed sense of self, a new me began to unfold. Although I continued to rely on the support of the spiritual sisters who had nursed me back to health; like a mother bird urging her newborn baby to leave the nest they quietly held my space as I ventured out on my own. As I reconnected with the elements of nature, a sense of longing like I had never felt before possessed me with a fervor that was all-encompassing. Every day became an adventure as I began to notice things that I had never noticed before. Mother Earth in all her glory unfolded in front of my very eyes. I now looked at the beautiful vistas available to me compliments of the Nantucket Sound with an immeasurable appreciation. Long walks on the beach provided ample opportunity to connect to a wisdom not realized in all of my younger years. As my path unfolded, the fire continued to burn.

Synchronistic to my journey, Dr. Wayne Dyer's book *Inspiration* became one of my first introductions to spirituality and the practice of leading an inspired life. Having no previous knowledge of Dr. Dyer, I had purchased his book as a gift for my mother knowing how she loved to read any type of inspirational book. Unfortunately, the onset of dementia quickly diminished her capacity to read so it no longer made sense to send her the book. I put the book back on my bookshelf thinking I would give it to someone else. One day as I was sitting at my desk, the book literally fell off my bookshelf and landed at my feet. Dr. Dyer is on the cover of the book with a butterfly sitting on his fingers. I was so attracted to the butterfly that I decided that I might give the book a quick perusal before putting it back on the shelf. Needless to say, I devoured the book from cover to cover and it ignited in me an unending thirst for spiritual knowledge. I began to read every book about spirituality that I could get my hands on.

Sometime after that, I was playing tennis on a beautiful spring day and I noticed that a Monarch butterfly was fluttering nearby. For some unknown reason, I quietly beckoned the butterfly to me by holding my hand out and saying, "Come here you beautiful butterfly." Much to my surprise the butterfly flew over, landed on my hand and sat there for what seemed like eternity. It was truly a magical moment and one I will never forget. The butterfly was fast becoming a metaphor for transformation in my life. One of my favorite artists and authors Kristen Jongen speaks of the butterfly in her book *Growing Wings*. In speaking to the metaphor of the butterfly she says, "What I have learned is the metamorphosis process is a choice. A caterpillar can remain a caterpillar for the entirety of its life, or it can risk the journey, totally deconstruct and have the faith that there are wings on the other side." It took several years and the shedding of many layers before my metamorphosis occurred.

My journey then became ongoing and my path wholly influenced by a heightened awareness of my authentic self. Those same intuitive thoughts that once appeared in my dreams unable to penetrate my daytime thoughts soon became a conscious part of my daily life. I was guided to form a company called *Inspired Ideas*, whose mission is to motivate other women to connect with their own inner guidance to bring transformation into their lives. I chose the butterfly for my company logo as that beautiful Monarch butterfly certainly contributed to my own transformation. I had witnessed grace that day in the purest sense of the word.

> **Surrender**
>
> *AFFIRMATION: All is well.*
> *I surrender to my inner guidance.*
>
> *Let go and let God. All is well. You don't have to do it all alone. Release negative thoughts about yourself, for your life is divinely guided.*

Not too long after taking the leap of faith to start *Inspired Ideas*, many things in my life began to fall into place. I was introduced to the Akashic Records which Edgar Cayce describes as a vibrational record of each individual soul and its journey. In becoming an Akashic Record Consultant and learning how to read the records, I am now able to connect my clients energetically to the full expression of their soul truth. Why are they here? What is their life purpose? With this new resource, I was ready and excited to reach out to a larger audience to offer inspiration and to provide an opportunity to others for healing and soul growth.

Last July, my neighbor and spiritual sister, Nicki Garner opened up the Angel Room Wellness Center, a healing cooperative on Cape Cod offering a variety of healing modalities designed to bring harmony and balance into people's lives. I was honored to be invited to become an Intuitive Life Coach at the center, working with an amazing group of healing practitioners. Last August, through yet another set of synchronicities, I was guided to Denise Linn's Soul Coaching program. The minute I pulled up her website, my heart skipped a beat and in an instant I knew that Soul Coaching was what I was supposed to be doing in this life. As grace unfolds, you go beyond even that little voice in your head that says "Go for it," and you move into a feeling of trust that everything is exactly as it is supposed to be.

"Have you lost your mind?" asked my outraged husband. You're going where to do what? "Yes that's right, I'm going to California next week to become a Soul Coach," I said. After three days of introspective contemplation, amid veiled threats of divorce, I decided to let fate or divine guidance play a hand in my destiny. I asked for a sign that would help me in making the final decision to register for the program. I pulled Denise Linn's website up for the hundredth time that week and clicked on the registration page. Staring back at me with big beautiful brown eyes was Denise Linn's dog Sadie. Sadie is an identical match to my own best friend and dog of ten years, Kayla. A rescue dog and mixed breed Basenji Terrier, Kayla has a very distinct face and markings. I had been given my sign. My husband didn't stand a chance after that. It was a done deal.

What I realized retrospectively was that once I finally claimed myself to the universe one hundred percent, my husband supported me even though he had no understanding of what I was doing other then the fact that it was important to me. After ten glorious days at Summerhill Ranch, I had found my calling in life. I was in love! My soul was singing. Finally for the first time in my life I knew what it felt like to be totally connected with the essence of 'who I am,' a spiritual counselor and facilitator of knowledge. I was really happy for the first time in a long time. As I felt the presence of grace in my life, I understood that grace embodies an awareness that does not require intellectual thought processing. It shows us "what is." It forces us to surrender to something greater than ourselves.

Grace allows us to truly see the light that is in ourselves and in each and every one of us. What is grace? I see grace unfold every time I look at my incredibly beautiful, intelligent and amazingly intuitive daughter, Christen. I see grace every time I get a glimpse of my exceptionally handsome, confidently soulful and musically gifted son Peter. I see grace unfold every day as these two priceless gifts from God continue to be present for me, even when I am not always present for them, and even when unwittingly I project onto them my own fears of not being good enough. I see grace unfold every time my husband of thirty-two years supports me in my spiritual practice even though he has no idea what it is I am doing and doesn't understand why I am doing it. For you see grace unfolds in the process of being present in your life. It is about being in the flow of what comes to us every day.

On this journey of awakening, I have learned to trust that my creator has given me all the tools that I need to live my happiest life. Mother Earth in all of her infinite wisdom provides amazing synchronicities to show us the way. The plants, the animals, the earth, the sky, the ocean, they all have something to say. It just takes being present to hear those messages. When you are truly in the flow you will notice that the people in your lives are also communicating important messages to you. They often offer you a magical mirror that allows you to see your whole self, the one with all of the faults as well as all the wonderful gifts you have brought into this world. You only have to observe. Remember there are no enemies, just friends and teachers. And finally when you are fully awake on your spiritual path, you realize that you are supported by so many amazing guides and teachers from the other side that are waiting for your call for assistance. Grace is all around us and it is in fact immeasurable.

In the words of the amazing Joan Erikson in *A Walk on the Beach*, ". . . our life cycles are our most creative effort . . . The struggle is to try and obtain a sense of participation in your life the whole way through." I thank God every day for the opportunity to connect with my divinity, the light within, to choose to be consciously awake and aware with each new step; to surrender to all of the possibilities that life has to offer. As grace continues to unfold, I find myself fully present in the moment, fearless and inspired to live the life that I have always imagined.

Remaining In Grace

As a Soul Coach, I am often asked by my clients if there is a conscious state of awareness associated with spiritual awakening. What is the significance of the signs and synchronicities that continue to appear in their lives? Should one move away from conflict and toxic relationships in order to find inner peace? Why do they all of sudden feel so disconnected from life? At first, it seemed like the best way to counsel my clients was to source information garnered from a myriad of books written by the most knowledgeable leaders in the New Age community. I became an authority on almost every topic relating to spirituality and the metaphysical.

Gradually, I realized that I could better serve my clients by tapping into the grace and inner wisdom that became increasingly available to me. I began to discover new sources for personal inspiration. I learned to trust that by acting only as the facilitator I could help my clients resonate with their own inner voice. A major aspect of Soul Coaching involves utilizing the four elements to assist in clearing and cleansing our physical, emotional, mental and spiritual bodies, affording a much greater connection to self. Here are a few of my 'pearls of wisdom' for optimizing health, claiming emotional integrity, gaining mental clarity and remaining perfectly in grace.

Mother Earth may not be our biological mother, but she is integral to the ongoing process of birth and rebirth on this planet. What I know is that in helping clients *optimize their physical health,* it is imperative to teach them how to align energetically with the forces of nature. Gratitude and respect for the sustenance and life force energy that is provided by Mother Earth is fundamental to this process. Through embracing a practice of daily gratitude, one begins to move with the flow of nature rather than against it. Eventually we become more present to the signs and synchronicities available to us as we attune more closely to our environment.

The Hopi Indians ask "What are your relations? Are you in right relation?" Our emotional well-being is interdependent on our relationships. What I understand is that we cannot compartmentalize these relationships. We cannot stay sheltered within the confines of a like-minded community and *claim emotional integrity*. It is in dealing with those toxic relationships and the daily interactions with family and friends that we honor our truths and afford the greatest opportunity for emotional freedom in our lives. As the flow of water remains the most important sustenance for daily living, so too does the flow of our relationships.

Perspective is as important as the air we breathe. It is what reconnects us with our divinity when we are seemingly lost. In the words of Oriah from *The Dance* ". . . show me how you turn away from making another wrong without abandoning yourself when you are hurt and afraid of being unloved." What I have learned is that by *sustaining mental clarity* in those moments, by breathing in fresh air and a new view, you can begin to lay the foundation for unimaginable growth opportunities. Engaging your mind, body and soul in a place of unconditional love of self and others is the fastest way to gain new perspective and by extension, new life.

We are all spiritual beings on our paths. What I have come to realize is that it is not about *being perfectly in grace* every day, but more importantly it is about being engaged in our daily lives. The greatest spiritual lessons come from falling out of grace day in and day out. It is in this process that we learn to accept ourselves with all of our shortcomings and all of our faults without judgment and without guilt. We learn to love ourselves fully and completely for all that we are. We come to understand that each and every one of us holds a piece of divinity within us. It is in this understanding that we can all shine our light on the world. It is in this process, that we learn that we are all teachers and we are all students.

✑

Bibliography
Northrup, Christiane. *The Wisdom of Menopause*. Bantom Dell, 2003.
Borysenko, Dr. Joan. *A Woman's Journey to God*. Riverhead Books, 2001.
Beattie, Melodie. *The Language of Letting Go*. HCI, 1990.
Jongen, Kristen. *Growing Wings*. Soul Soup Publishing, LLC, 2006.
Oriah. *The Dance*. Harper Collins Publishers, 2001.
Anderson, Joan. *A Walk on the Beach*. Random House, Inc., 2004.

Peace

AFFIRMATION: I breathe deeply, knowing that all is well in my universe.

Breathe . . . and breathe again, deeply, and often. Everything is flowing as it's meant to be, smoothly and effortlessly. All is in perfect harmony.

ROBERTA ASHKAWA BINDER
Black Mountain, North Carolina, USA

BORN AND RAISED in Eastern Pennsylvania, Roberta relocated to Colorado where she found a whole new world of research and exploration waiting. Native American Elders soon stepped into her life bringing opportunities for drum making, ritual, ceremony and myths to explode into truth. But the west was much too brown; her soul missed the green of Earth Mother that fed her creative vision.

In the mountains of Western North Carolina, Roberta loves how the trees change from the starkness of winter, to spring when tender buds peek shyly, then burst into delicate greens. The green slowly climbs up the mountains as the trees turn to shades of rich greens, appearing nearly black, as summer arrives. Fall comes and the leaves take on new coats of many colors, slowly dancing on the breeze to earth where they nourish the tree roots as all prepare for winter's sleep.

Roberta has incorporated her Feng Shui, Earth Energy, Sacred Geomancy and Space Clearing mastery into Eco-Friendly Feng Shui. Her studies have included Masters and Mentors from throughout the world. Additionally, both Oglala Lakota and Cherokee Elders continue to broaden her innate knowings of Earth Energies, Space Clearing and Energy Sensitivities.

As a Soul Coach, with a love of teaching and sharing ceremony, she facilitates retreats on such varied topics as Woman's Wisdom Studies to Goddess and Ritual getaways.

Roberta invites you to explore her website www.SacredEarthWisdom. com to learn more.

Fire – A Sacred Meditation

ROBERTA ASHKAWA BINDER

The Fire Ceremony can be done at anytime of the month, season or year.

*I*n my holistic studies I've discovered that many people are confused about the four directions and the elements associated with each direction. Fortunately I have had a group of Wise Ones to study with who always inspired individuality. Through their positive encouragement, I studied each direction and their many aspects and came to peace with the Calling of the Element Directions that resonate for me.

Growing up in Eastern United States, the Atlantic Ocean was to the east. And so my East has always been Water/Ocean. The Appalachian Mountains lay in the west of my home. And so my West has always been Air/Wind. The south was the direction of the equator and heat. And so the South seemed appropriate as Fire/Hot. The remaining decision was logical and easy; I lived in the north and was always connected to Earth Mother, so that presented Earth/Home. I add and always include, from my Cherokee and Lakota studies, and the Spirituality that I walk in, Spirit (the all): Father Sky, Mother Earth, All in-between.

With the gathering of Wise Ones who are represented in this book, you will find we each have different ways at looking at the same information. We are all correct. The main focus is to remain consistent in your Direction/Element assignments.

Earth – North
Source of all abundance, growth and fertility.
Many years ago I began a personal walk through the elements. The first element I worked with was Earth. I learned the Story of Earth Weaving from an Elder. When the ancient indigenous peoples left their home of origin they would take a small amount of earth from that place with them. That earth held the energy of home; the energy of generations of ancestors who had walked the now hallowed ground. And so it has been handed down – woman to woman, the gathering of the circle of generations of women through the energy of the earth.

The Story notes that this Earth Weaving tradition was also carried forth by the First People of the Americas as they traveled from home to home. These women took the tradition one step further by leaving a bit of the earth they had gathered in their travels from home site to home site – thus the joining together of the All or oneness.

This resonated with me and I began my gathering in Wisconsin. I brought along some earth from my then home state of Colorado and walked in quiet meditation with Spirit asking where earth was to come from. I asked three times and each time I was lead to the same location. And so my collection began. As my travels continued my Earth Weaving gathered momentum.

The following fall, I was honored to come together with twelve women from across the United States as one in a Circle of Wisdom. The piece I brought to the gathering was Ritual and bringing us to oneness. Each woman brought earth from her home place or a special sacred place near her home.

During the opening ceremony, each of us walked to the Bowl of All and we told a Story of the Sacred Place that we were uniting. We also added earth from the Earth of Place where we were meeting. Each day of our gathering as we opened our morning ceremony and closed in the evening, we incorporated our energies as we each stirred the Bowl of All. This energy built until our closing when we each gathered some of the united Earth Element to take with us to our homes, as a reminder of our Union in Wisdom. We then walked to the edge of Gold Lake and released the remaining earth to join with the waters – a piece of each of us remaining as one, now and forever with this place.

> ### Purification
>
> AFFIRMATION: *My energy field is being cleansed of all that I do not need.*
>
> *Cleanse your body and environment by doing space clearing, and shifting your clutter. Release whatever doesn't serve or support you in your life. Let go of the old, discarded, and unused; eat lightly; and consume fresh water and food with strong life force.*

Over the next two years, I continued to gather earth in my travels, and return some of the All to that locale. As my women friends traveled, I requested that they bring back earth from where they had been. The collection grew!

One July fourth, I dedicated my day to bringing the collection for all corners of the world together. It seemed an appropriate time as it was a time of declaring independence from the yesterdays and yokes of our places of origin.

I gathered all of the carefully labeled containers and one of my sacred bowls for the mixing ceremony. As each container was emptied, I held it, recognized the amazing woman who had gathered it, thanked her for her participation in bringing together the whole, thanked them for their role in my life, and thanked the earth for coming to me to be *United into the One*. It was a full and wonderful day and experience. Not only were the four directions coming together, the energy and elements of each corner of Earth Mother was represented in the Bowl of All. Peace.

I have shared this gathered earth with many Women Wisdom Keepers. They in kind, have shared the Sacred Earth with other Wise Ones. And the Circle of One continues to grow, uniting women around the world.

Although I continue to slowly grow my personal earth walk collection, I felt the union on that July fourth, completed my expanded world goal. Most recently I brought earth with me from the Fairy Garden at my Colorado home. It will be incorporated into the Fairy Garden I establish in my new North Carolina home.

Water – East
Leaping with joy, in waves of emotion, a container of healing buoyed up by serene peace.

I had begun quietly gathering water from Sacred Sites when I was first gifted with Seed Water from the Chalice Well, Glastonbury, England. At the time of the gift, I was completing my Feng Shui and Space Clearing Certification. A drop of this Seed Water continues to be frequently incorporated into the healing blends I use in my practice.

With this basis, I began personally gathering water samples from sacred sources in my travels and using them as seed water for the Sacred Ceremony Blends I create and in my expanding Ritual and Feng Shui/Space Clearing practice.

About this time, we were preparing for our second Circle of Wisdom Gathering. And once again, I was responsible for Ritual. This time our focus was Water. And so the source of our union became water from our individual home place.

Much the same as our original ceremony, each of we Wisdom Keepers brought Water of Place or from Waters that were near our home that we considered Sacred. It was an interesting collection, as some in our Circle brought tap water from home which they had blessed and others from a lake or stream nearby.

With our opening ceremony, we poured our individual Water into the Bowl of All and told its Story of origin. During our opening and closing Ceremony for each day, the stirring and unification of the Waters continued until our final gathering when the waters were divided among us. That Sacred Energy of our time together, our individual and now combined Source/Seed Waters became our new uniting link!

I find the Sacred Waters bring an additional boost of the Sacred of Their Place which is powerful and dynamic. Sometimes I will add some of my Sacred Earths to a blend or a complimentary crystal, hydrosol (the waters of essential oil distillation), or place the blend on a Word of Intention that I wish to incorporate into a ceremony.

I continue my personal Seed Water collecting as my travels take me to source waters. And these continue to be included in my Ritual and Feng Shui/Space

Clearing practice. Each bottle is labeled and they are all stored in a cool, dark location.

Air – West

Gently on the wind, filled with wisdom and song and the chance to soar, the wingeds glide.

To date air has been the direction that I have least explored. On the other hand, I have feathers I frequently use in Space Clearing and feather wands for use in Cleansing Ceremony. My Crystal Bowl resounds with its glorious voice resonating as it clears energies. I have certainly exercised Air's energy of Mind, as a lifelong student. I use the power of breath in my personal meditation and when guiding groups. I enjoy the stillness of the quiet Air, the gentleness of light breezes and at the same time marvel at the violence wind can hold in gales, tornadoes and blowing jet stream energies which push all weather flow.

Air brings me to thought, mental clarity, focus, creativity and inspiration as it is the direction of mind. We see it's manifestation in the spring with new life bursting forth and in the autumn with the falling leaves. It is captivating to watch the hawk gliding on its currents and witness the ripples dancing across the lake. There is so much to air . . . I look forward to that deeper exploration.

Fire – South

The flame dances passionately in the heat of the flame. It's warmth is felt in the noon day sun. Fire the creator.

As my walk evolves I turn to the Fire of the South. It is often bantered: "If you can't stand the heat, stay out of the fire." As this Fire adventure continues, I am frequently reminded of the full meaning of those words.

The healing energies of Fire have been acknowledged since those first two flints were rubbed together eons ago. Fire took food to a new dimension, one that most still follow today. Cooking meat killed many of the bacteria often present – raising the internal temperature beyond where those critters could survive. Many people still cook over an open fire . . . some call it barbequing, for others it is a way of everyday life.

One of my earliest Fire memories was as a child, about eleven years old, in the small Pennsylvania town where I grew up. There was a fire on the street that paralleled our home. This was nearly half a century ago; fire codes were very different; most of the homes were built of wood and easily went up in smoke. This fire raged; the flames shot into the night sky with vicious intensity. I sat in my bedroom window watching the leaping flames, sure that they would overtake our house. I mentally and then physically gathered the belongings that I considered most important for rescuing and stuffed them into two pillowcases, on the ready. It was frightening. The fire was put out with damage only to the single house. The next morning I put my treasures away.

As the years rolled by, I came to admire and honor fire. It has become my friend; a friend I hold in great respect. I've experienced fire in many ways: on the negative side with third degree burns from scalding hot water, on the positive side sitting around a campfire singing songs, drumming and listening to Story into the night!

Our most beloved ball of Fire here on planet Earth has to be Sun. What greater joy than welcoming Sun in the early morning, standing atop a hill and witnessing the beginning of a new day. The chill of darkness gradually replaced by the Sun's warmth as it moves higher in the eastern sky is a magical event and one that happens every single day . . . like clock work! Sun in spring brings forth the blossoms and buds that burst into flower and leaf. Sun in the summer melts the snow and causes the waterfalls to once again flow as the ice melts, warms the rivers, lakes and oceans and invites us to bathe in her warming rays as we play on beaches, wander in a meadow or park, or row quietly on a lake.

In the fall, as the days again grow shorter, Sun travels further from planet Earth and we start to feel the coolness and watch the trees, flowers and grasses prepare to sleep through the winter season. On the rare days when her warmth is bright, we are cheery and rush to enjoy the final outdoor days of autumn. When Sun shows her face in winter, we rejoice and give thanks for her shadows and light as they play across the bare landscape; we dream again of summer.

At the opposite end of the day, Sunset looms. My favorite place to say good night to the Sun is standing on a beach, the warm sand beneath my feet and the water quietly lapping at my toes. Silently the Sun just slips into the ocean's edge (or so it appears) and as it goes, it gives forth rays of glorious reds, oranges, yellows – a final gift as it tucks itself in, its journey complete with the part of planet Earth I'm standing on, but off to be sunrise elsewhere!

My second favorite treat at sunset is watching Sun disappear over the mountains. The interesting piece of that experience is how her light bounces back in reflection as she disappears to the other side. I never tired of watching sunset in Colorado as she headed over the Rocky Mountains. Sun's reflection often brought us an additional hour of daylight from spring through fall.

With the evolution of my Spiritual work, so too has come the evolution of my relationship with Fire. Candle energy plays a big role in all my work. This manifests in many magical ways. Simply sitting and concentrating on the flame of a beautiful beeswax candle can take one on adventures into life and beyond.

Color selection is important when you are working with candle magick energies. This can be manifested through the chakra colors when you are working with clearing a particular chakra. It can open gateways to understanding issues and in a sense burning them clear and clean.

At the annual gathering of the group Circle of One we make our new year Intention Candles. The tools are simple: a two-penny nail or awl, a pillar candle (three inches or taller works best), an essential oil blend, perhaps sparkles or a ribbon, whatever you would like to add for decoration (note if is flammable, you need to remove it prior to burning the candle). When selecting the candle color you might look at your personal year color, a feng shui color corresponding to what you would like to focus your year on: pink for relationship or perhaps pending marriage, black for building career and life foundation, red if you want to ignite your fame and reputation.

Coming together with a group of friends creates a jolly event to produce your intention candle; you can share your hopes and dreams for the year while engraving those intentions on your candle. Giggles and at times tears bring forth release and new ideas. We bring the remaining stubs of the previous year's candles, releasing the flames into the ether of intentions completed.

There have been other years when my intention candle has been done privately in the quiet, shared perhaps in front of a gentle fire in the fireplace. And sometimes an intention candle has been created in the middle of summer sitting in the backyard! It is all good and perfect . . . it is all about Intention and Blessing and lighting the Fire.

It is a rare ceremony that does not incorporate Fire. Following the Native American tradition, smudging is an important Fire used for cleansing and clearing prior to ceremony. This does not have to be limited to sage; I incorporate a large variety of herbs that I select for their appropriate properties for the work being done. These can include: Cinnamon for calling in money and abundance or to gain energy, Sandalwood to bring protection, to eliminate negative energies, Rosemary to enhance remembering and to purify, Cedar for purification and grounding, Birch to invoke Goddess energy, Oak leaves (dried) to bring inner strength, courage and hospitality, Apple leaves (dried) or seeds, to indicate the end of one cycle and the beginning of another. Apple wood is good to add to the Fire on New Years Eve; it is also used in any Fire ceremony that represents closing an era and opening a new one.

Fire is a spark of our life-force. It is the body temperature that we walk with each and every day of our lives. It is the inner temperature gauge that tells us we need a sweater to go outside, or if today is a day for sandals or a heavy winter coat for a snowy day. The internal Fire generally gets hotter when we are sick; we often think of a fever of burning out an illness. Fire is also called upon as the element to indicate the passion of Love, but it can also indicate the rage of anger, aggression and revenge.

Fire can wreak destruction (as in the Fire I witnessed in my youth or the forest Fires I became much too familiar with when I lived in the west), and yet, when the destruction of the raging Fire ends there is the renewal that follows in its wake. I remember being in Berkeley, California on the one year anniversary of a devastating wild Fire that destroyed many homes, and walking through the field of wildflowers that had sprung up in the foundations which were all that remained of home sites. It was beautiful.

Fire changes whatever it touches, never to return to the same configuration. That is a powerful thought that takes serious meditation to fully absorb and appreciate. Fire is considered Spirit. Fire is protector. Fire manifests as energy, warmth, and yet, Fire is also destroyer. Fire flares as rage and Fire symbolizes peacemaker through the sacred smoke.

Fire is often a Faith source. To the Chinese Fire is associated with yang energy – rising. In Judaism, Fire is a fundamental element that accompanies all offerings made to G_d. It is the image of G_d that Moses experienced in the burning bush, indicating in Hebrew that Fire signifies communication from G_d. In Buddhism, Fire often symbolizes forces such as desire, greed, hatred, and ignorance that remove a person from enlightenment. Releasing these Fires brings forth nirvana. And yet, Buddhism also uses the inner-flame to represent enlightenment. To Christians, Fire represents hope and life, serving as a reminder of the presence of God. In a Sacred Sweat Lodge ceremony of Native Americans, heat strips you down to your essence and the red hot stones begin to speak the ancient language of Spirit. In the Catholic and Orthodox Church, the tradition of burning incense continues today. Originally it was burned to kill the germs that people brought to services on their bodies (*and to protect the priests from those germs*). Today it continues as tradition and stirring ancient sacred memory.

Earth Mother was once a ball of Fire . . . to this day her core is still molten and fiery, sometimes breaking open in a volcano to pour molten lava over all that gets in the way of the flow.

Fire is autumn, when the leaves of the deciduous trees begin to dance with color: red, purple, orange, yellow and brown as they fall to the ground, another cycle of the year complete. Fire is experimentation and transformation. For the female it is represented in the lizard or snake; for the male it is represented in the thunderbird or phoenix.

Fire is Life, a Life that we are called to honor and greet with respect. When you start or see a Fire, show it the proper respect. Sprinkle tobacco or another sacred herb with gratitude. Never spit on a fire. Never drink alcohol or use recreational drugs around Fire. Never kick a piece of firewood. Never speak angry words around a campfire. Fire is a coming together in Love and Honor. In the Story of the Cherokee teachings, the first Fire was the beginning and every ceremony honors this Fire as the ancestor and elder teachers acknowledging Fire, with a reverence and almost mystical acceptance.

Fire takes and Fire gives. . . .

Creating a Fire Ceremony
Prior to doing Fire ceremony inside, it is best to practice outside – just to become familiar with the procedure. I would also suggest a fair amount of practice prior to using with clients.

The purpose for creating a Fire Ceremony is to release negative energy, to *burn it out*. It can also be a ceremony of completion. Some times when this is appropriate include, but are not limited to:

- After an argument with intense emotions.

- When moving into a new home, to release the energies of the previous residents.

- After a violation of your personal property (break-in).

- To celebrate selling a house and preparing it for new owners, or when a house won't sell to cut all remaining cords.

- Degree graduation from studies.

- It is also helpful for therapists and healers after working with a series of clients.

Tools you will need:

1. A small metal pot with feet or frying pan (I strongly recommend cast iron). Once you select your Fire pot, keep it specifically for this purpose.

2. A hot pad, bricks, or fireproof surface – the Fire pot will get *VERY* hot.

3. Epson salts or sea salt enough to cover the bottom of your Fire pot – no more than 1/8 cup.

4. Large wooden spoon.

5. Rubbing alcohol (no higher than 70%). I would suggest no more than 1/4 cup, just enough to easily cover your salts.

6. Matches (*A lighter could cause serious consequences with dangerous back fire*) – I only use wooden matches to drop in fire as you light the alcohol.

7. Potholder, the Fire pot will be hot.

Now that you have your materials gathered, prior to setting up the space:

- Set Intention. (I recommend doing this even for practice sessions; your intention would be to learn an appropriate ceremony for clients.) This will be the point of focus and called upon during your opening invocation.

- I keep all my tools in a sacred box; this way I don't have to scramble at the last minute when something is missing.

- In addition to the above list, especially when doing the ceremony for a client; set an altar. The altar pieces will vary with the intention and goal.

You are now ready with all your needed tools for ceremony:

- I would again revisit the Intention with clients – as you are setting the altar.
- Make sure all the windows and outside doors are closed.
- Call in the directions, asking the guides of each direction for help in the work that is about to be done.
- This complete, pour the salts into the bottom of the container – this does not have to be an exact measurement.
- Pour the alcohol over it (*replace the lid on the container that alcohol is in and remove it from the immediate area*).
- Strike the match and drop it into the Fire.
- Once that Fire is lit, never add anything more to it. Do not leave it. Do not move it. Focus on the flame; you can repeat a prayer, the Intention, chant – always keeping your focus on observing the flames. Watch until the Fire has burned out completely. You are honoring the Spirit of Fire as the Fire is honoring you. You will discover that each Fire will be different and with practice you will be able to *read* the Fire and what it is telling you.

Once the flame is completely out, use a pot holder to take the fire pot and release (scraping remains with the wooden spoon) anything that is left down the toilet. When the pot is cool enough, rinse with tap water as needed and flush until pot is clean.

Again return to the ceremony location and close the circle by thanking all the guides for attending and assisting. I generally talk to my client to see if they have any questions and/or comments, perhaps to share anything they saw or felt with the flames and to tell them what you felt or saw.

The Fire Ceremony can be done at anytime of the month, season or year. It is appropriate to use during the new moon energies for new beginnings and bringing in new energies; during the full moon energies for completion or releasing energies.

Respect Fire and it will likewise respect you. Always remember with the Element of Fire you can never be careless. Peace.

∾

PATTI ALLEN, M.A.
Toronto, Canada

PATTI ALLEN has a rich and varied background in the healing arts, education, public speaking, and writing. Certified as a Soul Coach®, Rubenfeld Synergist® (a form of body-centered psychotherapy), and Mentor, Patti runs a successful private practice using these tools to help people "grow their soul." With an expertise in dreams and Shamanic Dreamwork, Patti is also a Reiki Master and trained energy healer and takes a multi-dimensional approach to healing.

For ten years, Patti served on the teaching staff of Seneca College in Toronto in the field of Holistic Health where she has developed and taught the only course on dreams offered by a college in Ontario.

With a specialty in facilitating dream groups, she presents lectures and workshops on dreams. Patti holds a Master's degree in Humanities, where her research focused on dream healing in ancient Greece.

Patti has appeared as a frequent guest on television and radio where she teaches the public to work with their dreams. Most recently, Patti was featured in a 13-week television series called "In Dreams" and is currently a consultant for *Ghostly Encounters*, another W Network program. Patti was honored to serve as Mentor for Denise Linn's on-line training course through Hay House, "Gateway Dreaming."

Patti is most passionate about soul work and loves guiding others to use their dreams to access their inner wisdom. Contact Patti at www.PattiAllen.com

Dweller on the Threshold

PATTI ALLEN

I'm a dweller on the threshold and I'm waiting at the door.
And I'm standing in the darkness, I don't want to wait no more.
I have seen without perceiving, I have been another man.
Let me pierce the realm of glamour, so I know just what I am.

—VAN MORRISON

When we dream, we are all 'Dwellers on the threshold' keeping one eye on a dream door that transports us to another world, and the other eye on so-called waking reality. But the sense of waiting, of not quite knowing what is so, nor where we belong, has always accompanied this threshold. In dreams, we paradoxically find our selves in this liminal, in-between unreality that is *very* real. Yet we live in post-Freudian times and many of us grew up learning that dreams were the 'royal road to the unconscious.' And they are, but they are more than that. The first time I became aware that dreams were hinting at something larger than my own personal psychology was in an unlikely place for a revelation. The year was 1997 and I was sitting by the hotel pool on a very hot Philadelphia weekend. A family friend had just celebrated his Bar Mitzvah and my kids, numbering four, were cooling off in the pool along with all of Philadelphia it seemed. I sat in a lounge chair, watching the kids, watching people and reading Joan Borysenko's *Fire in the Soul*. In it, she wrote, "A Parable: Safe Passage Home." I read it and gasped. Then I cried under my sun hat. Somehow, in a few words, I found out why I was so interested in dreams, why I was a dreamer. Borysenko wrote:

The fledgling souls took many roads Home. Each Way had its own Story and each soul responded to that Story with the gift of free will, embroidering new stories on the dream-tapestry of the "One Great Dreamer."

With that sudden understanding, I could now see what wasn't there a moment before. In that moment, I reconnected with my Creator, with myself and to all dreamers in a way that I wasn't previously connected. Before, I felt like an orphan; now, suddenly, I belonged. Before, there had been an intellectual understanding of the psychology of dreams, now it was personal and it was spiritual.

In that moment by the pool I realized that I dream – *you* dream – because God dreams. Being "created in God's image," a familiar passage from the Bible, now took on deeper shading for me, as the idea took root in my heart and in my soul. Life was a noisy, hot day by a pool one moment and reality was where I had left it. Yet, a moment later, my eyes were opened to a broader perspective and I *understood*. I dream because God dreams! I was born of the One Great Dreamer and to dream is my birthright and my gift; it is both natural and supernatural. My fascination with dreams had come into alignment with the Creator. Yet this sudden spiritual awakening – my poolside *satori* – threatened to dissipate as I struggled to understand. Am I dreaming all of this? Am I dreaming my life? My children? (My deliberation paused as I counted heads in the pool.) If, like my Creator, I dream or create my world, are my own children, or anyone else for that matter, dreaming a different dream? Do common dreams create community and bind societies together? If my mind can play with the possibility that I've created my own reality, and I've dreamed this life of mine, then I have to also consider the possibility that God is a dream as well and who's dreaming whom? (And is it time to get out of the sun?)

So many of us who find our way to Soul Coaching are searching for the One Great Dreamer. My own search first led me to the world of dreams. I believed that if I could understand the message of a dream then I would gain self-understanding. I scratched below the surface of my dreams like a dog following the scent of a bone. At first, the reward was simply to understand myself. But when I started working with dreams, I realized that their special qualities and value didn't stop with me. At the core of the matter, was God. My search moved far beyond the need to understand myself, taking me into a world that was not visible to the naked eye, and where dreams were the technology for understanding both Self and Spirit. It is the same for those who embark on the 28 days of Soul Coaching. Dreams are the means, not the end and Soul Coaching gives us an itinerary and a route to follow. When we clear out the clutter in our lives, dreams give us another way of hearing the voice of our soul.

Dreamers have been looking for a route to spirit for many millennia. They often awake with a sense that they were dreaming *something* without being able to remember the details of the dream. We feel as if there is something we know that's just out of reach. This is not a new phenomenon. In Plato's *Republic* we learn of the Myth of Er, where we are told of the rewards, the punishments, the judgments that a soul encounters, the choices a soul must make and finally, of the River Lethe. It is this River of Forgetfulness of which the souls are required to drink, causing each to forget everything they had experienced prior to rebirth.

There is this belief in many cultures that we have forgotten our existence before birth. Judaism, too, tells of forgetting. In the Talmud it is told that before an infant is born the child learns the entire Torah (the sacred five books of Moses) in utero, but as the newborn is delivered, an angel taps the baby on its upper lip, causing it to forget (and thus explaining the indentation we all have under our nose, on our upper lip). Throughout the ages, there was a sense of there being something that we once knew but have forgotten. There is a word for it, *anamnesis*, which is a kind of remembrance, and means the remembering of things from a supposed previous existence. This idea shows up with little variation in medicine, religion and psychology as something previously known that is recalled to memory. So we spend our lives searching for what we suspect we've forgotten and surely, we'll know it when we find it. . . . Or will we?

In *my* own search to remember what I already knew, I was searching to find my way home, as Borysenko's parable tells us. I knew that there is a 'me' and a 'home' that will take me far beyond my ego and personality and ordinary life as wife, mother, Soul Coach and body-centered psychotherapist. But can we possibly remember the very thing we drank from the River Lethe to forget? If the angels have programmed us to forget, can we ever know God? Intellectually and academically, perhaps that was best left to philosophers and theologians to debate. Yet I was still left waking up every day from my dreams – or my life – wondering what I had forgotten.

All my dreams were woven into the foundation of who I was as an individual, just as we all bring the 'baggage' of our lives and our personalities to the process of Soul Coaching. My dreams had given me an awareness of my journey that I brought to my own Soul Coaching experience, but I knew that my journey was also being undertaken on behalf of my clients. As a guide, I can only be effective if I have walked down the road of psyche and soul growth myself. In my work, I had already been guiding clients on their own journeys (although I didn't call it that) when they came to me in a psychotherapy or healing session. But Soul Coaching provided me with a structure for what I was already doing intuitively. This work does not focus strictly on contemplation and silence as a way to connect with the Creator as many programs do. While these are important tools to use, Soul Coaching connects people with themselves *and* their creative/God source, so that body, mind and emotions all become an important part of the spiritual mix. Soul Coaching, with its use of the four elements, provides a multi-leveled and grounded approach that is unique.

Perhaps like me, you are looking for an encounter with your authentic Self, Spirit and healing. I began my Soul Coaching training with an unspoken belief that if only I could gather the right combination of tools, I would succeed, right? Self-pressure? Magical thinking? You bet! And I might as well admit to one of my more challenging personality traits: When it comes to myself – and *only* myself – I am a perfectionist. For all the personal self-growth work I have done on myself for the last two decades, clearly I wasn't finished! I still had three issues weighing me down, one more literal than the other – weight and body image, writing and the issues of belonging – and my demands for self-perfection were wreaking havoc with all of them! Just like the baggage that we all bring to new endeavors, I began my Soul Coaching training with expectations firmly in place: Professional skills will be honed, Spirit will be encountered, weight and body issues will be vanquished, issues of belonging will be clarified and my writing will be unblocked. A tall order indeed!

Many of us bring this impatience to the Soul Coaching experience. 28 days to enlightenment? Great! In a world of instant gratification, I couldn't transform fast enough and I had already learned many of the skills in previous trainings. Impatient as we are, this work reminds us that we don't uproot a newly planted seedling in order to see how it's doing. Soul Coaching reassures us that change and growth are indeed afoot even when we aren't yet aware of them. "It's happening" is the Soul Coach's mantra and we ask you to be patient with yourself. We learn to trust this process by letting the process unfold in its own time. But sometimes it is our impatience that colors our expectations and our experience. In my case, I impatiently waited . . . and waited. It wasn't until Day 22 in Earth week when I had a transformational conversation with each part of my body that began the alchemical process of change.

The exercise was to give each body part a personality and from that point of view, tell myself what that part wanted me to know. My parts all had something to say once they knew I was listening! Here's what my too fat hips had to say: "All you ever do is complain that I'm so fat, big and wide. But I'm built in that traditional goddess build. I'm made for belly dancing, lots of fabric, flowing material and lusty nights. Get over society's no-hips obsession because you won't ever be that! Start moving me Sister, and groove in my ability to rock and roll. Get me some goddess-wear skirts too!" And from my lungs and my heart: (I wrote, "I'm afraid you will fail me like you failed my father and my grandmother who died of lung problems.") My lungs replied, "Because we failed them, and they failed you? See the connection? If you see us through the eyes of a wounded victim we could fail you too." They said, "See me as we are – your source of vital life force and breath. Disconnect your victim thinking from us, and fill us with air and love and give us Reiki from time to time. We won't fail you." To which my heart added, "You are so afraid that I will fail you too, but fear does not help me to be strong and clear. Love does. Send me love. Open me and send me love to myself. Watch the inflammation you fear be countered by love and healing energy. It's time."

Day 23 was a busy one for me so I didn't do the exercises in depth. But Day 24 sealed the transformation as I made major connections. It was indeed happening but I hadn't even begun the exercises for the day! I was up at 3:00 that morning, and when I couldn't go back to sleep, I decided to listen to one of Denise's meditations to slow myself back down. I put on "Clearing Negative Programming" from her *Past Lives and Beyond* CD. By doing that meditation, visiting one past life after another, I realized that I don't hate my body! I found that my weight issues were actually the result of my core beliefs around belonging; that I don't "fit" in. There were a lot of life-long and past life examples and beliefs that confirmed this. I discovered that even my hesitation to write is related to this too. I've either felt or been wrong or alien or different or just didn't fit in, or tried to fit in the wrong mold, and suffered simply for being who I am. I didn't fit in – I still don't fit in – and I felt that to my core. At the same time, the meditation helped me realize that I wasn't a misfit, but a perfect fit for me! Intellectually, I realized that 'fitting in' is over-rated, but really *feeling* that isolation with my body, mind and spirit, set me on my healing journey. Now, through the Soul Coaching process, I was getting ready to release this habitual way of seeing myself.

> ### Sanctuary
>
> AFFIRMATION: *I am divinely guided gently and lovingly.*
>
> *Go within and find your inner refuge.*
> *Be a safe haven for others.*
> *Step forward with grace, deliberation,*
> *and thoughtfulness. Take moments*
> *for reflection.*

Whatever preconceived notions we bring to the Soul Coaching experience, if we can let go of our need to get the answers that we want, the process unfolds for each of us in the way we need. The three most stubborn issues that I brought to my Soul Coaching journey, the issues of belonging, writing, and my weight, all came through loud and clear, in their own time. It really was happening! Now the work of reframing began and I found new ways to be around people and food and still fit perfectly with myself. I found a way of eating that agrees with my body and constitution, though it often has me eating differently than everyone else. It's not without ups and downs, but for the most part, I learned that what I thought was an issue of hating my body, was really an issue of belonging. Rather than my body, what I hated was the result of not being in alignment with myself. I began writing too, though still in fits and starts. My perfectionist was the last hold out.

The 28-Day Program culminates with a Quest and I still had to do mine. The Quest, whether one hour, one day or more, always gives meaning to the Soul Coaching journey. Like many Baby Boomers, my life has been punctuated by the music on the radio. I grew up listening to the Beatles and Rolling Stones, went to my first dance with Aretha Franklin teaching me how to spell, and learned to drive with Steppenwolf's "Born to Be Wild" blasting on the radio while I exceeded the speed limit. My Soul Coaching Quest had a soundtrack as well.

> *Ring the bells that still can ring.*
> *Forget your perfect offering.*
> *There is a crack, a crack in everything,*
> *that's how the light gets in.*

—LEONARD COHEN

Leonard Cohen seemed to be writing the lyrics for my Quest, though I only saw it once I had completed it all. The synchronicities that led me to this song

(Anthem) wove itself in and out of my week. The sun shone on Toronto that day and I started my Quest by going for a walk in the ravine across the street. I saw no wildlife; no birds appeared, though I could hear them, nor did my beloved hawks that frequent the ravine make an appearance. Slightly disappointed in that, I did notice three beautiful spider webs, shimmering in the morning light and dew. I thought of the creativity and language associated with spider in Native traditions and felt that the nudge to write was in that encounter as well as the mystical associations with the number 3. As I walked I noticed a lot of snails on various plants, but not on the ground where I typically see them. I was reminded how the snail travels with his home on his back, and like him, everything I need is within me. So my new refrain, "I fit in perfectly with myself" joined in with the Quest.

I returned to my home office, where I had already smudged, clearing the energy with dried sage. I set up my circle with crystals and feathers, and other objects that had meaning to me. And I rang the bell that I received in my Soul Coaching training ["So ring the bells . . ."] trying to make the perfect offering. ["Forget your perfect offering . . ."] I prayed, I meditated and during those few minutes – perhaps twenty minutes or so – I lost awareness of my body. . . . When my self-awareness returned (not knowing where I had been) I felt like moving, so I did. Slow, adagio, twisting, turning. . . . I tend to be quite self-conscious about dancing and I don't do that very easily if someone is watching, so it was interesting that when I was alone and safe in my sacred space, my body clearly wanted to move. I put on some angelic music and let it move me. Then emotion flowed as I spiraled and released old energy from who knows where. It felt like an emotional colonic but I knew from my work as a body-centered psychotherapist that there was an intimate connection between body, mind, emotions and spirit, so I let it flow!

The birds they sang at the break of day.
Start again I seemed to hear them say.
Do not dwell on what has passed away,
or what is yet to be.

When I sat down, everything was distant and detached and I felt that I stood outside my usual point of view. As I looked around at my space, filled with objects that I love, they were now empty of meaning, without desire or attachment for me. None of this felt bad or pathological at all. It felt surreal and I was just the observer, noticing with distance. Remembering my body conversation on aging and death, I wondered if this was what it was like to die. That suddenly our emotional attachment dissolves and we know this was just a scene in a play, albeit a play we were fond of, where the parts we inhabited were not who we really are. All the things that mean so much and seem to matter so intensely while we are focused on our lives, are dissolved as illusion in a nano-second.

Then I don't know why or what thought preceded it, but I put on Leonard Cohen's song, on my ipod. There is something to be said for a Quest with technology! And now it was as if he was blessing my Quest with his words. And I cried some more. Forget your perfect offering. There is a crack. *I* am cracked. We are *all* cracked. And if I admit it, allow the imperfections to be, the light enters and I am 'en-lightened.' But the paradox is that we are all enlightened already, if we could only see ourselves that way. Like my little snails, it is all there and even the cracks, too, are illusion! Take *that* my inner Perfectionist! Then I remembered a dream I had:

I am on stage in an open amphitheatre, and there is something I am supposed to do but I don't know what it is! I seem to be an honored guest. Then a crow flies overhead and I point and say, "Look. A crow. It's a good omen."

And that was it; my job. All I had to do was read the signs! So that synchronistic song that had already arrived the week before, made it's way into my Quest, paving the way for the connections I would experience and the insights that would unfold. As it wove with this old, remembered dream, I realized that's all that I do. I read the signs. And every day, every moment, every dream is a Quest. It's all there for you too, if you keep your eyes and ears and heart open. And when you lose your way,

Start again . . .
Do not dwell on what has passed away,
Or what is yet to be.

These are instructions for life, pure and simple. For me, I finished that Quest shaking with the connections I made and the letting go that resulted. Then I showered . . . and started again.

In some small way, I might say that my life is the story of one woman's journey and search to remember the dream she had of herself, of God and of all creation, all while cooking dinner, raising four children, and doing work that she loves. And this chapter is a record of that journey – my field notes from the road because as I write this, I am still searching and still dreaming. I am a "Dweller on the Threshold" with one foot in the dream world and one foot on the ground of daily life with its pleasures and its pains.

Ironically, the more I dwell in the dream world, contemplating its insights and adventures, the easier it is to access its wisdom and guidance as I find my way in the waking world. I've seen the reports of other dreamers and I know I'm on the right path, tracking my Self and Spirit, however many potholes and detours I encounter. We are all Dwellers on the Threshold with a foot in both realms, but who has the courage to step over the threshold? Dreamers do. And Soul Coaches guide them.

A Dreamer's Tools for Soul Coaching

Dreams can have many levels of meaning. If you take the time to remember your dreams, work with them and lovingly draw out their meaning, you will see that these levels of meaning correspond with the four elements of air, water, fire and earth. This makes them the perfect complement to the deep work of Soul Coaching.

Air

The element of air corresponds to the mental realm. Dreams reflect your attitudes and beliefs from your waking life. As well, they will often show the dreamer where a course correction in those attitudes can be made. Air or wind, as a symbol, will point to issues of thought and attitudes or messages from Spirit, for many dreamers.

Water

The element of water corresponds to the emotional realm. Working with your emotional life is one of the best uses of dreams. Dreams will tell you exactly how you feel about any given subject, even when you are not aware of those feelings. Dreams of water are often symbolic of emotions or spirit, and the type of water or the circumstances surrounding it can give the dreamer useful information.

Fire

The spark of life, passion, purification, anger can all show up in a fiery dream. Fire corresponds to the spiritual realm and the type of fire, the details and the circumstances will point the dreamer toward its meaning.

Earth

The element of earth corresponds to the body and the physical realm. The earth in a dream can symbolize Mother Earth, our physical home, issues of the feminine, of grounding, as well as pointing to the dreamer's physical health.

Using Dreams with Soul Coaching

- In addition to a process journal, keep a record of your dreams as you catch them, starting on day #1 of the 28-day Soul Coaching Program. If you are new to dream catching, your intention to remember and record your dreams will take you most of the way there. Be sure to leave your journal and a pen next to your bed for easy recording. Too much movement can yank you right out of that delicate dream space.

- Mark each dream with A (Air), W (Water), F (Fire) or E (Earth) according to the predominant element in the dream. Many dreams will have more than one element. At the end of each week, see which elements are in the majority and ask yourself the following:

Mostly Air Dreams – What ideas or beliefs are reflected in my dreams that I need to change or let go of to live in alignment with my heart and soul's desires?

Mostly Water Dreams – What emotions do I need to work with, release or transform in order to live in alignment with my soul's plan for my life and my relationships?

Mostly Fire Dreams – What passions or creative energies might I develop or allow if my soul called the shots? What fears are holding me back?

Mostly Earth Dreams – What messages predominate in my Earth dreams? What physical way can I remain grounded yet fluid in my life choices? What does my body want me to know about it, and is it in alignment with my soul's plans for my life and my health?

- On day # 7 of each week, review your dreams from that week and choose the strongest dream or dream symbols on which to meditate. For example, if you have some powerful dreams with healing symbols in Earth week, meditate on these symbols and imagine them infusing your body with health and wellbeing.

- Ask yourself: If my dreams had a message for me, directly related to what I have learned this week, what would it be? Do the symbols or messages complement what I learned this week or clash with them?

- Do my dreams suggest that any changes need to be made to my life's direction? If so, what action can I take or what changes can I make in order to honor the dream?

- How can I walk in alignment with the messages of my dreams and my soul? What do I need to do differently to change the energy and direction of my life? Take a fresh look at the messages in your dreams and with the "beginners mind" of a Zen master, create some new ways of meeting old challenges.

In dreams you have an easily accessible tool for understanding self and spirit, and with relatively little effort, you will be rewarded with rich and vibrant messages. As you mine your dreams for their precious jewels, you may find that you have an inner Soul Coach available to you every night. Sweet dreams!

LINDA J. STEWART
St. Louis, Missouri, USA

LINDA STEWART inspires and empowers you to connect deeply with your essence and nurture soul-expression.

As a spiritual teacher, writer, consultant and coach, she offers a unique and innovative approach combining Soul Coaching®, sacred psychology, evolutionary astrology and feng shui. She mentors and supports your inner journey and assists you in creating a home that reflects your essence and nourishes the deep contentment of living in harmony with your soul.

For most of her life, Linda has been a seeker. Her quest for meaning and purpose has inspired her journey into unknown places within herself to gain self-knowledge and understanding. On her journey, she found Soul Coaching®, a powerful resource that taps into the vast landscape of inner wisdom.

Linda holds a degree in Psychology and professional certifications in Interior Alignment™ Feng Shui and Soul Coaching® and has studied many healing modalities including Evolutionary Astrology, Shamanism, Reiki, Healing Touch and CranioSacral Therapy. Years of personal experience coupled with a wide array of education gives her a distinct advantage in helping others . . . she has walked the talk.

Linda's gift for nurturing is transformative and enduring. Her gentle, sincere and compassionate nature, deeply intuitive insights and ability to listen genuinely are her hallmarks. Whether she is helping you deepen your relationship with your self or creating environments of beauty and harmony, her intention is to inspire you to live joyfully . . . to celebrate who you are!

For more information contact Linda at www.Linda-Stewart.com

A Soul-Nurturing Home

LINDA J. STEWART

*As we create a home for our soul, our essence shines brilliantly,
becoming a beacon of light for others as well.*

The rain is pelting on my windshield as I merge into rush hour traffic. It has been a long and trying day. My shoulders are up to my ears and my jaw is tightly clenched as I grip the steering wheel and concentrate intently on the dark, glazed road ahead of me. The gnawing headache that has pulsed at my temples all day is intensifying. The cars are creeping along in slow motion. Thankfully, I don't have far to go. I continue to inch ahead hoping it won't be long.

Crawling around the bend, my exit comes into sight. I push my body forward in my seat magically hoping my effort can somehow get me there sooner. The cars continue to crawl at a snail's pace. Just a little longer and, finally, I reach the exit. I turn off the main thoroughfare and snake through the side streets. As I make my final turn, I see a warm glow from the window and hear the gentle tinkling of the angel wind chime beckoning me forth. I can almost hear a soft whisper offering a cheery welcome. "Come in," it says. I begin to feel the tension drain from my body. I breathe a sigh of relief. I am home.

"Home sweet home." "Home is where the heart is." "There's no place like home." We've all heard these expressions many times. They touch a place deep within us. We feel the tug of 'home' at our core. Why are our homes so important to us? What is it about 'home' that evokes this profound yearning within us?

In essence, our home is a primary source of nurturing for us. It tends to us every day, satisfying our needs for shelter, safety, security, belonging and rejuvenation. Home is a sanctuary embracing us as we unplug from the stressors of daily life, a place where we can truly relax and just be. It is a womb that nourishes and supports us, a nest offering comfort and encouragement on our life journey.

At a deeper level, our home is a reflection of our self, a physical expression of our inner being. The furniture, colors, accessories and placement of objects express our uniqueness. Like an autobiography, the days of our life are engraved in our home. As we look around, we see our life story. We identify with our home and are intimately connected to it. Our home is much more than a building of walls and a roof, or a group of rooms serving different functions. It is a sacred space . . . a temple for our soul.

Since we spend so many hours of our life there, our home exerts a powerful influence in shaping us. If we keep everything the same in our home, we have a tendency to remain the same. We don't see anything new. When we make changes in our home to declare who we truly are, we awaken to the splendor and beauty of our soul. When we make changes to assert what we are seeking, we open to new opportunities and possibilities. Seeing is believing. Seeing our aspirations depicted in our home helps us to believe they are possible.

The ultimate goal of the Soul Coaching program is to align our inner spiritual life with our outer world. What better place to start this process than in our home? Because our home deeply influences us, as we make changes in our home to express our essence, our life begins to resonate with these changes. We experience the deep peace of living in harmony with our soul. We feel the sense of 'home' within.

Radiance

AFFIRMATION: I am a radiant reflection of God's light.

Your radiance acts as a beacon pulling the bounty of the universe to you. Your heart is open, your spirit glows, and your connection to the Source is strong.

Each week of the Soul Coaching program is dedicated to one of the four elements (air, water, fire and earth) offering exercises and activities related to each element and the part of us associated with this element. The final week focuses on the earth element. After spending three weeks clearing mental, emotional and spiritual clutter and listening to the messages from our soul, the earth week centers on our physical world. This week is devoted to nurturing our self and our body, our physical environment, and deepening our connection to Mother Earth. After releasing old negative beliefs, habit patterns and emotions that no longer serve us, we are ready to move in the direction of our dreams. It is time to take the invisible (our essence, values, desires and intentions) and bring it into physical form. It is time to align our inner spiritual life with our outer life. It is time to create a home for our soul.

Nearing the end of the journey, Day 26 focuses specifically on this. I have found the practice of creating a home for one's soul so powerful and significant that it has become the essence of my work and my mission in the world.

The first time I journeyed through the Soul Coaching program, I became aware that my life purpose is to nurture and heal. Of course, this means that I nurture and heal myself too. Tending to me by creating a soul-nourishing environment has been an integral part of my spiritual journey. As I designed my home to comfort and soothe myself, I felt more self-love and compassion. As I made changes in my home to reflect who I am, I felt a deep appreciation for the beauty and elegance of my soul. As I created my environment to cultivate my gifts and talents, I found myself easily and naturally expressing them. As I aligned my home to resonate with my spiritual center, I felt a sense of 'home' within. The most exciting part of this whole process was how much fun I was having. Creating a soul-nurturing home is *fun*!

As a Soul Coach and Interior Alignment™ Feng Shui practitioner, I help others remember their magnificence and create a home that nurtures and inspires the soul's expression. When I work with a Feng Shui client, I do so in the spirit of a Soul Coach. Who is this person? What does he or she value? What nurtures him or her? How can I help this person express his or her talents and gifts? The most important part of my work is helping my client gain self-knowledge so I can help him or her create a sacred space that truly expresses and cultivates this unique essence. The fun begins as I witness my client opening up to his or her soul. Maura is a good example.

When I entered Maura's apartment, the first thing I noticed was the color and creativity emanating from the room. As we talked, Maura explained that she was majoring in psychology at a local university but struggling with her decision. She was at a crossroad, unsure of which way to turn. She needed direction. Could I help? Maura's eyes lit up and her face relaxed as I asked her questions about herself. The more we talked, the more excited she became. She told me that for fun, she had recently begun to take art classes but believed she wasn't very good. As we walked around her apartment, I noticed several paintings leaning carelessly against the dining room wall. They were remarkable . . . passionate, dramatic, vivid and beautiful. I asked her about the paintings and to my surprise, she told me that she had painted them. I was stunned.

"You are an amazing artist!" I declared. She recoiled in disbelief not wanting to see her talent. As we talked, I encouraged her to hang her paintings in her apartment. Again, she hesitated saying she felt awkward, uncomfortable and boastful, but the gleam in her eyes told me the truth. "How about hanging just one when you're ready?" I nudged. She was willing and soon after our appointment she hung one painting on her wall for the world to see. As we worked together over time, I continued to help her create a home that truly mirrored her soul. Recently, I had the honor of attending an art show where her paintings were highlighted. She has graduated from a prestigious art school and is creating her life as an artist. When Maura hung that first painting on the wall, it was a powerful and defining act. The passion and creativity of her soul was free to shine.

Change begins with awareness. When Maura became aware of her remarkable artistic talent by seeing it daily, she was able to design a life that fostered her soul-expression. Just as Maura found and cultivated her path, you can too. There are four valuable and effective steps to creating a soul-nurturing home: 1) increase self-knowledge, 2) evaluate your home, 3) remove blocks to soul-expression and

4) express your essence. The use of a journal will be helpful for the following exercises.

1) Increase Self-Knowledge

The first step in the process is getting to know your unique and precious soul. Just as a child needs time and attention to grow and thrive, your soul does too. Taking time with the following exercises will help you become intimately acquainted with your self.

- Answer the following questions in your journal: Who am I? What do I value? What are my interests? What brings me joy? What are my gifts and talents? What are my aspirations? What do I yearn for? What is seeking expression in me? You may want to concentrate on these questions as you go through your day jotting down the answers as they come to you. Be mindful and observe during the day what you are drawn to as you seek your answers. If you want to explore more deeply, working with a Soul Coach and the Soul Coaching program are excellent resources.

- Write 10 words or symbols that define who you are. This suggestion comes from Alexandra Stoddard in her book *Feeling at Home: Defining Who You Are and How You Want to Live*. For example, my words are – love, flowers, beauty, nature, color, books, light, the moon, journals and home. Next to each word, write why this word defines you. To take it a step further, ask a close friend or family member to write 10 defining words as they see you. You may learn something about yourself that was previously unknown.

- Make a collage with the theme "Who am I?" Cut out words and pictures from magazines, calendars, etc. that appeal to you. When you are finished, hang your collage in a well-traveled place in your home so you see it often. Step back and look at it with fresh eyes. Why did you choose each picture or word? What do they convey about you?

- Take a soul journey. The soul journey is a wonderful way to learn things about your self that may be hidden or forgotten. These 'buried treasures' are gifts from your soul.

Close your eyes and bring your attention to your breath. Begin taking slow, deep, cleansing breaths observing the air as it gently flows in and out. Continue until you feel relaxed and peaceful. Next, bring your attention to your heart center, the hearth of your soul home. Visualize or imagine you are walking into your heart center, to the very core of your soul. Your soul center could be a room, a place in nature, or whatever comes to you. Once you are there, ask your soul if it has any messages for you. Ask your soul to tell you something about your self that will help you gain self-knowledge and self-understanding. Give your soul time to express what it wants to say to you. Spend as much time here as you need. You may want to ask more questions. When you are finished, thank your soul for its love and care and very easily and gently come back to the here and now. Note what you learned in your journal.

2) Evaluate Your Home

To help you recognize where you are right now, the second step focuses on assessing your home.

- The Life/Home Assessment: List 5 words or phrases that describe my life as it is now. How do I feel about my life right now? List 5 words or phrases that describe my home. How do I feel about my home? What does my home represent to me? Is there a connection between what I wrote about my life and my home?

This exercise increases your awareness of the connection between your life and your home. Is your home a metaphor for your self and your life?

- Answer the following questions about your home in your journal: Does my home reflect who I am today (based on my findings from the first step)? What in my home inspires me to express my gifts and talents and realize my dreams? What gives me a sense of peace? Do I feel loved and tended to in my home? Am I comforted and soothed there? Do I feel safe in my home? Does my home nurture me? How do I feel when I approach my home? Does my energy rise, fall or stay the same? In what room(s) do I feel the best and why? Is there a room or place that brings my energy down and why? What does my home say about my level of self-care?

After completing these exercises, you will have a better understanding of where you are so that you can begin to make conscious choices that reflect and cultivate *you* and the future you desire. You may be feeling overwhelmed or discouraged right now. This is part of the process. When you gain awareness, you begin to see the difference between what you desire and reality. It is very helpful to get support during this process. Whenever you make changes in your life, the support and encouragement of another person infuses you with confidence to continue on your path. As your Soul Coach and Interior Alignment™ Feng Shui practitioner, I support, nurture and encourage you as you walk in the direction of your dreams.

3) Remove Blocks to Soul Expression

To create a soul-nourishing home, it is imperative to remove items that are life-negating and depleting. Thus, the third step involves eliminating anything from your environment that causes physical, emotional, mental, or spiritual stress. This 'clutter' is draining to your spirit. If you don't love it, need it, or use it, the item is an obstacle to soul-expression.

Physically, this could be furniture with sharp edges that could cause injury or a droopy, half-dead plant that saps your energy every time you walk by. Emotionally, this could be an item kept that was given to you by someone who treated you badly which is a daily dose of criticism and thus harmful to your self-esteem. Mentally, this could be broken items or too much stuff which keeps you in a state of overwhelm and stagnation. Spiritually, this could be things that no longer represent you, keeping you mired in the past and unable to express your potential. Clearing your home clears your life as well. Removing obstacles allows the natural radiance of your soul to sparkle and shine.

- What room or area in your home is the most bothersome to you? This is the best place to start because by clearing and cleaning this one area, you will gain the maximum reward. It is similar to the 80/20 principle in business. 20% of the clutter causes 80% of the upset and frustration. Even if you do one small thing at a time, the effects will have an enormous impact on your life force energy.

- Make a list of ways you can nurture yourself. Include activities, experiences, people and places that nourish you. Place this list in a well-traveled area in your home so you see it every day. Add to the list whenever you discover something new.

If this exercise is difficult for you, you are not alone. From my experience in working with people, many are unaware of what truly nurtures them. I've had students in my classes admit that they simply don't know. Sometimes it helps to pretend you are offering suggestions to a friend. What suggestions would you recommend? Write them on your list. Another idea is to write a description of your perfect day. The activities and people in this description belong on the list.

Having a lot of 'clutter' is an indication that you need nurturing. Instead of focusing on the stuff and how overwhelmed and frustrated you feel, change your mindset to what nurtures and comforts you. The more you focus on nurturing yourself in a healthy and loving way, the more secure and happy you will feel and less likely to accumulate stuff.

4) Express Your Essence
In the fourth step, you are the artist and your home is your canvas for soul-expression. Expressing your essence in your home does not have to be costly. As your creative juices flow, you will discover simple, innovative and economical ways to intentionally design a space that resonates with your soul.

- Based on what you learned in step one, what additions or changes can you make in your home so that it reflects you? An easy place to start is with the ideas from your '10 word' list. What are your words? Find a way to express them in your home. This simple act of finding tangible ways to express your soul will bring you immense joy, inspiration and satisfaction.

For example, one of my words is 'the moon.' I have always been attracted to the moon and I especially love the full moon. Many years ago, when I began to study astrology, I realized why this was so. First, I was born when the moon was full. Second, in my natal chart, the moon is placed prominently at the midheaven in the tenth house, i.e. the house of career. I am a strong lunar person with gifts of nurturing and healing. I express my lunar gifts in my work as a Soul Coach and Interior Alignment™ Feng Shui practitioner. Placing a lunar calendar and a picture of the phases of the moon in my office has helped me to own and express my gifts and talents in my work.

My client, Emily, found the soul journey helpful in this process. Emily is a very talented woman who is active in many endeavors. She has spent the last thirty years tending to her family. Her youngest child had recently graduated from high school and was preparing to attend college away from home. Emily was entering the 'empty nest' phase of her life and was fearful and reluctant about her future. I invited her to begin creating a home that reflected herself and her husband and the new life they were embarking upon. I asked her to choose something that represented herself and to place it in the center of her home. She expressed having difficulty knowing her self beyond her roles as wife and mother and didn't know what to place in this area. I could see she was struggling, so I offered to do a soul journey meditation with her to help her connect to her soul and hear its messages. Emily eagerly agreed and before I uttered another word, she had already closed her eyes.

When she entered her heart center during the meditation, her deceased father was at the door to greet her. They sat on the old brown couch she had as a child and talked. She had been very close to her father and felt a deep fondness and connection to him. They were a lot alike, sharing similar qualities and interests. Through the soul journey, she felt the closeness and joy of being with him again. Afterward, she told me that since his passing, she had hidden objects that were reminders of him to ease the pain and grief of his loss. She was floundering as she tried to construct a life without him.

During her journey, she realized how much she missed him and that she was ready to bring out the 'buried' items. While talking, Emily went to a kitchen drawer and unearthed a beautiful hummingbird statue hidden under a mound of papers. The hummingbird had been a gift from her father. When she was a young girl, they enjoyed the ritual of watching hummingbirds visit the kitchen window feeder. Emily placed the statue in a prominent position in the center of her home. We continued to talk about other interests and qualities they shared and found ways to express them in her home. Displaying these items helped Emily connect to those parts of her self that seemed to die with her father.

- What inconsistencies or discrepancies did you notice from doing the exercises in step two? Did you find that your home does not reflect who you really are? Did you find that it is unwelcoming? Did you find that your home does not encourage you to express your gifts and talents? Did you find that your life and home aren't reflecting what you truly yearn for? Make a list of the inconsistencies. Decide which one bothers you the most and take action. What changes can you make in your home so it is in harmony and alignment with who you are and your aspirations? Making these changes is an affirmation of support, encouragement, and love for your self.

My client, Charles, found that he yearned for fulfilling and meaningful work yet he had a dead-end job and was tired and listless most of the time. In assessing his home, I found the desk in his office was tiny and filled with stacks of papers and unfinished projects. In Feng Shui, our desk is symbolic of our work. It was a defining act for Charles to purchase a beautiful, large oak desk in a style that made his heart sing. It was a clear message to his soul that he and his work are valuable and important. Since then he has changed careers and is doing work that brings him joy.

- Increase the nurturing quality of your home. Just as a seed needs light, fertile soil and air to germinate and grow, your soul seed needs cultivating as well. Go to your list of ways to nurture your self from step three to get ideas. For instance, what people are nurturing to you? Place photos of them in your living room as daily reminders of their love and support. If flowers are on the list, treat yourself to a bouquet regularly. If reading nourishes you, design a comfortable and cozy nook to do so. Make every room in your home a place where you feel tended to and cared for.

When nurturing yourself in your home, remember the bounty of Mother Earth. Including nature in your home is profoundly healing, soothing and uplifting. A picture of your favorite natural setting, a bowl of fresh fruit, or an exquisite amethyst crystal imbue your space with nourishing energy and honor the beauty and grace within you and around you.

Designing a home that truly nurtures us is a powerful spiritual practice. When we take the time and energy to create a bedroom that is restful, warm and soothing, we feel valued and appreciated. When we choose things that express our inner being, we honor our soul. When we maintain and tend to our home, we are in essence tending and caring for our self. When we truly respect and love our self, our home reflects this. It sparkles with radiance, vitality, inspiration and affection. The love that emanates from our home blesses and welcomes us each time we enter its doors.

Creating a soul-nurturing home is a new way to live; a fun and joyful way to shift our reality. Instead of staying stuck in past hurts, difficulty and suffering, we can consciously construct a template that honors and cherishes us. No matter what has happened, we can begin anew. A soul-nourishing environment can be our biggest supporter as we stand at the brink of the rest of our life ready to step forth into our future. Like a mother waving to her child on the first day of school, our home cheers us on, nudges us forward and encourages our growth and development. It feeds our soul.

The deepest longings of our soul are to be seen and heard. When we express our soul in our home, our home mirrors our essence back to us. When we enter our home and see our soul, we feel a deep sense of connection, belonging and acceptance. We feel seen and heard. This is a powerful act of self-love and self-regard . . . of being present with one self.

The more we feel 'at home' in our environment, the more 'at home' we will feel within our self and the Universe. As we create a home for our soul, our essence shines brilliantly, becoming a beacon of light for others as well. Loving and nurturing our soul through our home becomes a way we can make a better world for everyone.

❧

Bibliography
Linn, Denise. *Soul Coaching*. Hay House, 2003.
Linn, Denise. *Feng Shui for the Soul*. Hay House, 1999.
Stoddard, Alexandra. *Feeling at Home: Defining Who You Are and How You Want to Live*. HarperCollins, 2001.

SOPHIA FAIRCHILD
Sydney, Australia

SOPHIA FAIRCHILD is an international author, editor, writing coach, spiritual teacher and publisher.

Sophia grew up around Australian aboriginal people, saw faeries and spoke to angels as a child. Her Irish great aunts and Aboriginal great grandfather profoundly influenced her intuitive gifts, playfulness and love of storytelling.

She is a certified Soul Coach®, Past Life Therapist, Gateway Dreaming™ and Space Clearing practitioner, personally trained by the remarkable Denise Linn. Sophia is also a Faery Intuitive, Professional Spiritual Teacher and Angel Therapist®, certified by Dr. Doreen Virtue, Ph.D.

Both a seasoned writer and award-winning editor, Sophia's stories have appeared in many publications, including *Soul Moments*, also published as *Coincidence or Destiny*, edited by Phil Cousineau, foreword by Robert A. Johnson, Conari Press, 1997, *Traveler's Tales: Tuscany*, Traveler's Tales Guides, 2001, *Angels 101*, by Doreen Virtue, Hay House, 2006, *Angel on My Shoulder*, Malachite Press, 2007, *The Miracles of Archangel Michael*, by Doreen Virtue, Hay House, 2008, *Soul Whispers, Collective Wisdom from Soul Coaches around the World*, 2009, Soul Wings® Press, *The Healing Miracles of Archangel Raphael*, by Doreen Virtue, Hay House, 2010 and in *The Wisdom We Have Gained*, edited by Kim Pentecost.

Look for the next book edited by Sophia Fairchild ~ *Angels: Winged Whispers ~ True Stories from Angel Experts around the World*, 2011.

Sophia lives in Sydney, Australia, where she teaches regular seminars.

www.Soul-Wings.com

For editing and publishing services contact her at Soul Wings® Press.

www.SoulWingsPress.com

Weather Whispers:
Beyond the 28 Days

SOPHIA FAIRCHILD

When we collaborate with each of the four elements, including the weather,
to restore inner and outer balance, we bless everything in Nature.

I was born on the hottest day of summer and my son was born during a winter blizzard. Like most people, my memories connected to weather-related events hold far greater intensity. Extreme weather events fill us with awe and act like huge wake-up calls. They remind us that the natural elements have a direct influence on our lives, that we are deeply connected to the natural cycles of our planet and to all living things.

Like many young girls growing up in remote communities in rural Australia, I spent a lot of my childhood away, shut up in boarding schools, seldom allowed out into the wilds of nature to experience the exhilaration and freedom of connecting with the elements. It was considered a privilege for aboriginal girls from Outback Missions to be shipped off to such educational institutions. But through being cut off, not only from our families, but from our beloved wide landscapes, we all suffered from a similar dis-ease – Nature Deficit Disorder.

I recall escaping one night through a high, narrow bathroom window, down a two story drainpipe, and out into the mystery of a mid-summer night. Magical moonbeams illuminated the quiet landscape, allowing me to roam, to touch and inhale the fragrance of exotic blooms, throw my arms around ancient trees and feel their deep blessing in return.

My heart exploded with joy at being able to take off my shoes and feel the texture of the rich, moist earth caressing my soles. In the still, sacred space of that mystical night, I fully embraced being completely immersed in nature. The sudden realization came to me that nature never sleeps. It is alive, full of small creatures and elemental activity . . . all the time!

As I drank in the silence, punctuated by sweet calls of night birds, the owl's low swooping flight and the rustle of baby birds stirring in their nests, I became aware that 'sacred space' can be anywhere that feels holy to us, that Nature herself is a temple for the soul and we are privileged to be cradled within her bountiful arms.

I was just a small, homesick child, but in that moment I experienced the comfort and support of every aspect of nature, including a host of shimmering Nature Spirits. Escaping into the wild freedom of that moonlit night filled my innocent child's heart with a sweet awareness that has never left me – that Nature is a living system which we are all part of, and which is *responsive* to us.

So, how can we escape our media-dense modern lives, where virtual realities have caused so many of us to suffer from Nature Deficit Disorder? No matter where we live, one of the easiest ways to connect more deeply with nature is to become attuned to the dynamic weather patterns all around us. Each of the weather elements is part of the story of life cycles in nature. All are necessary to support life here on earth. And because we are all connected and part of this living world, everything we do affects every-thing and every-one else in the world, including the weather. As human beings, we are not only caretakers of our planet but conduits of loving energy, which we can offer in support of the balance of all of the elements in the living world around us.

Owing to the wind's ceaseless circulation –
over a year's time you have intimate relations with oxygen molecules
exhaled by every person alive, as well as by everyone who ever lived.

—GUY MURCHIE, *The Seven Mysteries of Life*

Too often we curse the weather, never fully appreciating the blessings of its many moods. Once, following a busy conference, I found myself standing out in a gale in the twilight of the town square of a small Greek Island, trying to call my insurance company back home on my cell phone. There would be no flights out now for a week due to a freak storm. All the shops and tavernas were battened down against the tempest, so there was no shelter. I had nowhere to sleep and hadn't yet located my luggage after the evacuation from the small airport.

Just then, a hurricane-force gust hit the village square, and for a moment I was flying like Dorothy in the Wizard of Oz! While airborne, the wind blew all of my travel documents out of my hands, up and away into the night. Touching back down to earth I braced for a crash-landing. Instead, like Mary Poppins without an umbrella, I danced lightly across slippery wet marble and came safely to rest.

The last piece of paper I'd seen flying away into the dark sky was my 'World Time Calculator.' Time was no longer important. I'd already missed all my flight connections to get back home and it would be days now before I'd even arrive back in Athens. I was left with my passport, cell phone and a credit card tucked into my blouse. In fact, the storm left me with everything I needed to gently return home, including a suspension of time.

Life is lived much more fully when the rules of normal time no longer apply. Some days later in Athens, after a series of soothing sea voyages, I had plenty of time left over for a serene sunset visit to the Parthenon (which I'd previously missed in my rush to get to the conference) before my rescheduled flight home. That storm gifted me with a much-needed 'time out' to reassess my priorities, instead of rushing back to a hectic routine. Life is a gift to be celebrated!

It is said that every cloud has a silver lining. Recently, after a devastating tornado had flattened their town, a small Kansas community rebuilt everything using the sustainable principals of wind and solar power. It's true that whenever we're forced to rebuild, we're always given the opportunity to reshape our lives in a new way, with stronger foundations. And if we watch and listen, Nature always provides us with inspiration for the way forward.

All the water that will ever be is, right now.

—NATIONAL GEOGRAPHIC, OCTOBER 1993

Life on earth would cease to exist if there were no rain. Yet the affect of floods can be life-changing in many different ways, for everything in their path. One Christmas Holiday, I watched my entire collection of plastic Walt Disney characters floating away in the rushing brown waters of a killer flood, along with shoes, books, clothes, snakes, cattle, cars and houses. It was the turning point of my adolescence. I knew in that moment my childhood was over. Anyone who has ever lived through such massive floods knows how precious and precarious life can be.

Yet even destructive floods can be a gift to those living downstream. This year, late summer cyclones brought flooding rains to the north of Australia. These flood-waters moved inland to swell vast empty river systems and dry lake beds, breaking a severe drought. Through the miracles of Mother Nature, plants and animal species which had lain dormant for more than fifty years sprang back into life. Enthralled Naturalists traveled from all over to witness the spectacular diversity and abundance of wildlife teaming around newly created Outback Lakes.

The Chinese . . . designate 'the wise' by a combination of
the ideographs for wind and lightning.

—HERMANN KEYSERLING

The mystical qualities of lightning, related to the Fire element, have been recorded in myth and legend throughout the world. The Greek God Zeus was known as the lord of lightning, and in Norse mythology Odin's hammer evoked lightning and thunder. As with all the weather elements, Fire can both create and destroy.

The *Wandjina*, the Dreamtime Ancestral spirits of Northern Australia, bring the annual monsoonal rains that gift new life to parched summer lands. I've seen painted stories depicting the Creator Being, the Rainbow Serpent, and the Lightning Brothers who create Lightning, at spectacular rock art sites in the remote sandstone ridges across the Top End of Australia. Stories that are tens of thousands of years old tell us that the *Wandjina* have special powers, and if offended, may cause intense lightning storms and flooding. These rock paintings are still believed to contain powerful energy and should be approached with caution.

As small children, my older sister and I were brushing our long hair before bedtime during a severe tropical thunderstorm. With each brush stroke we noticed crackling sparks coming off our hair. Suddenly, a floating sphere of Ball Lightning appeared at the open window. It hovered there for a moment, then shot across the room and out the opposite window. This floating globe of white lightning left the room with a strong smell of ozone and our hair standing on end!

To this day I'm still fascinated by lightning. Neither the scientist, nor the shaman can fully explain it. Only lightning knows what lightning is. It demonstrates and explains itself to us through action. Through enormous flashes of energy, lightning breaks down nitrogen in the atmosphere which then combines with oxygen to form nitrogen oxides. These are carried to the earth's surface by rain, instantly enriching the soil and turning everything green. Lightning creates natural fertilizer out of thin air. Magic!

Mandala means circle . . .
the basic motif is the premonition of a center of personality,
a kind of central point within the psyche, to which everything is related,
by which everything is arranged, and which itself is a source of energy.

—C. G. JUNG

Traditional sand painting designs are still created by Australian aboriginal elders as part of important seasonal ceremonies. I was once encouraged by an aboriginal friend to attend the creation of one such sand mandala at a large art museum in Sydney, though I hadn't yet been introduced to any of the artists. These sand paintings in desert ochres depict powerful Dreamtime stories, creating a direct link with the Ancestor Spirits.

When I arrived at the gallery that afternoon, I was told by the staff that the Aboriginal exhibition would not be opening for another three days and that the area was closed to the public. But my friend, who lived far away, had known exactly when the ritual sand painting would be created. She had said "They'll be doin' it as the sun goes down."

It was closing time when I walked past the security guards into the Aboriginal wing of the big art gallery. There, I was greeted by the Aboriginal artists like an old friend. They shooed away the flustered security people saying, "We know her. She was invited," though I had never met any of them before.

I sat with the aboriginal elders, watching the huge sacred painting take shape in red sand on the floor of the deserted art gallery in the center of the city. As they sang the traditional chants of the ancient creation story, a fierce lightning storm began to rage all around us, triggering the gallery alarms to echo through its empty halls. They had sung to the lightning spirits, and the lighting spirits had spoken back.

Just as a candle cannot burn without fire,
men cannot live without a spiritual life.

—BUDDHA

The word kundalini comes from the Sanskrit word for 'serpent power.' Activation of the kundalini, the 'inner lightning,' occurs when the divine feminine Shakti, or life force energy, moves from the root chakra up through the spine to the crown chakra, where it unites with the Shiva, or male polarity, at the top of the head. Kundalini has been termed 'the solar principle in man' by philosophers from Plato to Hermetic alchemists, and the experience of kundalini rising is known as the 'baptism by fire.'

Years ago, after an afternoon of blissful meditation in the spectacular Kalahari Desert, followed by a night of trance dancing with a family group of Khoi San Bushmen, I felt the spiritual fire rising. This experience lasted three full days. My advice to you if the spiritual fire begins to rise within you is to seek support from a shaman, or those experienced in energy work, to assist you in gently moving this explosion of energy back down into the heart chakra. There are many accounts of people who've taken years to fully recover from a prolonged kundalini experience. It may require considerable focused effort to settle the energies down to where normal life is once more possible.

> **Beginnings**
>
> AFFIRMATION: *I cherish all the cycles in my life.*
>
> *A new cycle is beginning in your life. Wipe the slate clean; it's now time to release the old and start again.*

The kundalini experience is ecstatic and transformative, though for some people it may be difficult to readjust to ordinary life after such an explosion of bliss. Spiritual fire remains mysterious, similar to lightning. Much like an inner volcano, it is a powerful eruption of life-force energy, light and visioning, which brings unexpected blessings, but which may also be damaging in its intensity. As with all fire, it deserves caution and respect. And yet, like fire itself, it is a gift beyond measure.

Weather Working

Studies have shown that a group of people concentrating on one thought at the same time can influence the weather, just as prayer has been shown to have a positive effect in healing. Thus we all have the ability to influence the weather.

In indigenous cultures, weather-working is traditionally part of the shamans' responsibility to maintain the health and well-being of their communities. We've all heard of Native American Rain Dances to bring rain. In Tibetan culture, certain monks have the duty to produce the blessing of rain for specific religious ceremonies, or of preventing it for others. Even today, this ancestral link to ancient practices of weather working remains in many parts of the world, including Africa, Australia, New Zealand, Polynesia, Asia, the Americas and Europe.

However, everything regarding weather-working has a 'down wind' effect which can have unforeseen consequences. Therefore any attempt to produce weather modification contains the risk of undesirable or harmful results for those living downstream.

I was living in Malibu, California at the time of the Los Angeles Summer Olympic Games of 1984. As the summer heat arrived that year, so did the smog. Though we were young and inexperienced, a group of my friends decided to attempt a ceremony to clear the smog, so the Games would not be affected by the usual unhealthful Smog Alerts.

We lit a small fire on the beach as the sun, symbol of the balanced Fire element, set into the ocean. We then focused on drawing moisture from the one tiny cloud in the sky. Southern California has a desert climate so it rarely rains at all during the summer. Mysteriously, though no precipitation was forecast, overnight it did rain lightly. We awoke to blue, smog-free skies, which remained clear for the rest of the Olympics.

During one terrifying wildfire season in Southern California, we were forced to evacuate with just our photo albums and the cat. Before departing, I visualized our home completely enclosed by a pyramid of white light. Upon our return next day, we discovered that a forty foot wall of flames had roared down the canyon, burned everything around our property, then leapt across the road to destroy forty-three homes. Miraculously, our house was still intact.

People are often prompted to work with the weather elements during a time of damaging wild fires. Here I must caution you. Be very careful what you ask for. It's better to focus your energies on *balance* and *protection* than to beg for rain. The water elementals may answer your prayer too enthusiastically and bring floods instead of the calm, moist air, most beneficial in halting wildfires. Always visualize balance between the elements, rather than the opposite weather extreme.

We must walk lightly on the earth, be gentle on ourselves and harmless towards our neighbors.

It's easy to create your own simple ceremony to Bless the Weather, or any part of nature you feel needs rebalancing.

First bless and give thanks to the Land. Acknowledge the Ancestors and request their assistance as you set your intention for balance.

Call on the Deva of the Land, Spirits of the Four Directions, the Four Elements, the Spirit within, the Archangel of Healing, and any Nature Spirits who wish to work with you.

Close your eyes and imagine a sphere of radiant green light at the center of the Earth, rising up through the earth, enfolding you in a shimmering ball of green light, surrounding, nurturing and protecting you.

Then imagine a sphere of warm, white light coming down from the shining Sun above, enfolding you completely in golden-white light, the radiant light of the heavens.

Now imagine these two spheres of light meeting together in your heart, creating a beautiful, shimmering light like a star, whose sparkling rays radiate all the way back down into the center of the earth, and all the way back up to the heavens above . . .

Now breathe this light back into your heart until it forms a glowing sphere of golden-white light.

On the out-breath, send this light out into the world as a blessing of love . . .

The Nature Spirits know how to work with this blessing, to direct it anywhere in the world where extra support is needed to restore harmony.

Now fill yourself up again with this golden-white light . . . holding your connection to All That Is for a few moments . . . And when you are ready, allow yourself to return, filled with gratitude.

And so it is.

> *Go Walkabout.*
> *Go alone.*
> *Have no itinerary.*
> *Listen to the spirit of the land*
> *through the soles of your feet.*
>
> —KALKADOON ELDER, QUEENSLAND

If the Earth Element within us is neglected or out of balance, we cannot be truly effective in any aspect of our human experience. One of the great benefits of answering the call to pilgrimage in my own life has been the opportunity to gather in the energies of all the other elements, to ground them into my earthly body. Being fully grounded is essential to our spiritual, psychological and physical well-being, and to our ability to give our soul full expression as a gift to the world.

To follow your star on a pilgrimage (exposing yourself to the elements) is a time-honored way of getting in touch with the Earth element. It is also a way of sharing a silent blessing with the world.

Many of the major ley lines on our planet follow ancient pilgrimage routes. The Camino de Santiago de Compostela trail through Europe to the Spanish Coast and the pilgrimage of the Magi to visit the Christ Child in Bethlehem are both examples of pilgrimage routes that follow the stars.

The ancients were led by the patterns in the night sky – the Milky Way, the North Star, the Pleiades or the Southern Cross. Thus the patterns of the stars were 'traveled' on this earth. In Australia such spiritual trails, or cosmic stories reflected in the landscape, are called Songlines.

In Africa, tribal people will lie down on the trails left in the earth by animals to receive earth healing. The Africans believe that wild animals follow lines of energy, or what we call ley lines, within the earth's surface. But perhaps they too are navigating by the stars.

It would seem there is a complex link between energy lines on earth and the patterns in the heavens, creating a kind of mystical union between heaven and earth. The geometry of all the pyramids, stone circles and sacred sites on this planet reveals that all are sited on major energy crossings, and all are related in some way to the patterns of the stars, the sun or the moon.

There is a pilgrimage of the heart in which we are a gift,
giving ourselves from the inexhaustible richness of our Souls.

—DAVID SPANGLER

Whenever we are present to the journey, we are on a pilgrimage. Such sacred journeys serve to fulfill our yearning for mystical union.

While some of us are called to physical pilgrimage by heaven and earth (the stars or the sacred sites), others are called to walk the sacred labyrinth. Many will travel a similar path through their hearts while taking the Soul Coaching journey though the elements. All are sacred pilgrimages of the soul.

Just as Nature blesses us with a living temple for our body and spirit, when we collaborate with each of the four elements, including the weather, to restore inner and outer harmony, we bless everything in Nature.

Thus the gift is reciprocated.

Vision Walk with the Weather Elements

As wild landscapes around us disappear,
being in nature helps ignite the wild, mystical landscapes in our souls.

—DENISE LINN

Following the 28 days of your Soul Coaching journey, you may wish to embark on a spiritual retreat or Quest in nature. Even a short Vision Walk can be experienced as a sacred pilgrimage or mini Quest.

Take a quiet walk in a natural setting, opening yourself up to the wisdom of each of the Four Elements. During this personal pilgrimage, pay close attention to how the elements are expressing themselves through the weather around you.

A Vision Walk involves moving with reverence, quietly holding the intention of receiving new insights, while remaining open for messages and signs.

The purpose of your Vision Walk is –

• For soul renewal and to give blessings

• To connect with each of the Elements and corresponding Nature Spirits

• To find out which of the Four Elements can assist you most right now

• For inspiration, illumination, grounding, and blossoming into your true Self

• To create a New Vision for your life

Use the suggested questions and elemental correspondences below as a guide, or feel free to create your own.

Air
Direction – East[1]
Represents – Intellect, perception, intention, communication, poetry, connection to life force
Archangel of Air – Raphael, *Healer of God*
Season – Spring
Intuitive Gift – Clairaudience
Nature Spirits of Air – Sylphs
Weather Extreme – Hurricane, Cyclone, Tornado
Visualization for Balanced Element – Clean Air, Refreshing Breeze, Rainbows

Questions:
From which directions do our winter winds come? Or cooling summer breezes?
How does Wind affect me personally?
eg. Does the wind give me a sense of freedom? Does it help me to clear my thoughts?
What message does the spirit of the Air Element or Wind have for me?
Remember to be grateful for the clean air you breathe.

---

1. The elemental directions used here are derived from my Celtic Ancestry and apply to the Northern Hemisphere. If you live below the equator, the elemental associations on the wheel reflect seasonal opposites.

Fire
Direction – South
Represents – Energy, transformation, inner strength, passion, fertility, connection to personal power
Archangel of Fire – Michael, *He who is like God*
Season – Summer
Intuitive Gift – Claircognizance
Nature Spirits of Fire – Salamanders
Weather Extreme – Heatwave, Wildfire, Volcano
Visualization for Balanced Element – Sunrise, Sunset, Contained Campfire

Questions:
When were the last wild fires here, and how did they effect the environment?
How does the element of Fire affect me personally?
eg. Does its warmth and light inspire me to be creative? To play and dance?
What message does the spirit of the Fire Element or Lightning have for me?
Remember to give thanks for the Fire that lights your way.

Water
Direction – West
Represents – Intuition, feelings, purification, music, emotional release, inner reflection, compassion
Archangel of Water – Gabriel, *Strength of God*
Season – Autumn
Intuitive Gift – Clairvoyance
Nature Spirits of Water – Undines, Mermaids
Weather Extreme – Flood, Blizzard, Tsunami
Visualization for Balanced Element – Soft Rain, Deep Pool, Calm Sea

Questions:
Where does the water I drink come from?
How does the Water Element affect me personally?
eg. Does it feel good to walk in the summer rain? Do I feel better after crying?
What message does the spirit of the Water Element or Rain have for me?
Give thanks for the purity of the water you drink.

Earth
Direction – North
Represents – Grounding, ancestors, material foundation, ceremonial dance, connection to life path
Archangel of Earth – Uriel, *Light of God*
Season – Winter

Intuitive Gift – Clairsentience
Nature Spirits of Earth – Gnomes, Dryads (tree spirits)
Weather Extreme – Drought, Earthquake
Visualization for Balanced Element – Stable Soil, Fertile Garden, Old-growth Forest

Questions:
Could I easily create a calendar of the seasonal cycles where I live?
How does the Earth Element affect me personally?
eg. Do I feel nourished and full of life force? Does the earth help me feel grounded and secure?
What message does the spirit of the Earth Element have for me?
Give thanks for the Earth which nourishes your body and soul.

Creating a New Vision
When creating a new vision for your future, it's helpful to work with all four elements combined, in a balanced way. The Weather Elements provide us with a direct encounter with each element as an expression of nature, and can add fascinating new dimensions to this process.

Through Air/Wind our thoughts are cleared and we perceive the new idea; through Fire/Lightning we receive the Divine Spark, the call to action and the creative inspiration to move forward. Water provides us with emotional intensity, the necessary desire and motivation to proceed towards our dream. Earth enables us to manifest our dream by grounding it into reality. Once we have integrated all four elements, the fifth element of Spirit becomes activated, breathing new life into our vision, allowing us to birth our gift into the world.

∽

Blessing

During and after your Soul Coaching journey, be aware of the magic and power of the four elements to produce profound changes within you, and in the world around you, to create balance and harmony within all things.

Remember to honor the gift of the elements, and the elements will honor you.

We wish you many blessings as you journey through the secret alchemy of the elements . . .

Deep peace of the air to you as you breathe in new life.
May wisdom flow to your ears.
Deep peace of the water to you.
May the stillness of the deep pool reflect in your soul.
Deep peace of the sun to you.
May you feel its warmth in your heart.
Deep peace of the earth to you.
May strength and serenity be yours.
Infinite peace to you now,
and forever more.

—ADAPTED FROM *The Dominion of Dreams* BY FIONA MACLEOD

Light

AFFIRMATION: My light radiates through my life and the world around me!

You are the light, and you come from the light! You illuminate the world, so rejoice and remember who you are. You have a physical form, but that's impermanent. At your source, you're luminescent! Lighten up . . . don't take things too seriously.

Editor's Acknowledgements

$\mathcal{H}$eartfelt thanks to all of the amazing Soul Coaches who've shared their soulful wisdom and professional expertise throughout the pages of this book. Your dedication to the path of the soul is truly inspirational! We also wish to thank the authors' friends and families for supporting them on this journey. Many thanks too, go to Kelly Chamchuk for proofreading assistance and Fiona Raven for adding her magical vision to these pages.

Immense gratitude from us all goes to Denise Linn for allowing us to use excerpts from her *Soul Coaching Oracle Cards Guidebook*. Denise, your good humor, wisdom and love are blessings received and returned by us all. Finally, special thanks to my son Marlon, whose enduring love and encouragement brings laughter to my soul!

About Soul Wings® Press

Publishing for the Soul®

Soul Wings® Press is an award-winning Small Press Publisher.
We specialize in providing compassionate, professional editorial services
and quality book publishing to assist experts in the fields of
Self-help and Spirituality to become published authors.
www.SoulWingsPress.com

Soul Wings Press® Titles
of related Interest

Soul Whispers: Collective Wisdom from Soul Coaches around the World 2009
Angels: Winged Whispers – True Stories from Angel Experts around the World 2011